SOCIAL FACTORS IN ECONOMIC DEVELOPMENT

The Argentine Case

AN M.I.T. RESEARCH MONOGRAPH

TOMÁS ROBERTO FILLOL

SOCIAL FACTORS
IN ECONOMIC DEVELOPMENT

The Argentine Case

THE M.I.T. PRESS

MASSACHUSETTS INSTITUTE OF TECHNOLOGY
Cambridge, Massachusetts

1961

FOREWORD

M.I.T.'s Brooks Prize, named for E. P. Brooks, the first Dean of the School of Industrial Management, is awarded to the best Master's thesis submitted during the year to the faculty of the School of Industrial Management. In 1959–60, the Prize was awarded to the thesis submitted by Tomás Fillol, a graduate student and Master's candidate in the School of Industrial Management. This monograph, adapted by Fillol from his thesis, also has the distinction of being the first Brooks Prize thesis published in what we hope will become a useful series in the industrial management field.

Fillol's thesis seeks to make a contribution to our understanding of the relationship between the social and economic environment of a country and the shape and character of its developing industrial organizations. He analyzes Argentine social and political structure as it has influenced the development of a management style and the concomitant union leadership reaction in the context of economic development. In this, he raises useful questions not only for appraising Argentine industrialization but for the general case of industrialization in a less developed economy.

It is significant that the first Industrial Management thesis published in this series should be in the international field, a growing area of significance for American management and for students generally interested in industrialization and economic growth.

HOWARD W. JOHNSON
Dean, School of Industrial Management
Massachusetts Institute of Technology

PREFACE

This monograph is based on *Industrial Relations in the Economic Development of Argentina,* a Master's thesis submitted to the School of Industrial Management at the Massachusetts Institute of Technology in May 1960. The original study has been thoroughly revised and the order of chapters changed. One full chapter, dealing with the history and present status of Argentine trade-unionism, has not been included in this book. Four other chapters—historical studies of the Argentine economy and of the nation's social transformations, an analysis of Argentine labor legislation and social welfare programs, and a survey of today's labor relations — have been summarized and incorporated in this monograph as part of the general exposition.

The author is perfectly aware that one of the chief criticisms to which this work will be subject is that the concepts and assertions contained in it — and especially in Chapter 2 — are based on records of individual experiences and tentative generalizations, rather than on a scientifically devised investigation. Preconceived theoretical assumptions are here blended with opinions and casual observations, and the result presented as factual conclusions without any systematic attempt at empirical verification. The impossibility of devising even the smallest representative sample in connection with the material here expounded is obvious. However, in order to remedy to some extent these shortcomings, the opinions and observations of other authors and investigators have been cited wherever possible.

The author expresses his deep gratitude to Professor Charles A. Myers, Director of the M.I.T. Industrial Relations Section, who gave every encouragement, precious time, and the benefit of his advice and experience first as thesis advisor and subsequently in reading the manuscript; and to Professor Everett E. Hagen, who read the original draft of the manuscript and most of whose many helpful suggestions and criticisms were included in its final form. The author is also indebted to Professor Edgar H. Schein, who read the thesis manuscript and made helpful suggestions at various stages of the research and writing.

Tomás Roberto Fillol

Cambridge, Massachusetts
September 1960

CONTENTS

ix

1 INTRODUCTION

Economic development cannot be conceived solely in accounting and mechanistic terms, as the transfer of capital and plant, the switching of factors of production. It proceeds through the refashioning of aptitudes, habits and personal relationships, the creation of new forms of co-operation and organization, the generation of new goals for individuals and for communities. It is a social process in the sense that every member of society is involved in the fashioning of new social structures which co-ordinate the action of individuals for the attainment of new goals. The economic and technological and the social aspects cannot be separated, for capital is embedded in the institutions and customs of the people and changes in technology require the creation of new types of human organization. We must therefore consider economic development not merely in terms of the problems of planning by a relatively small group of government and business people, but as the work and the problems of millions of people trying to create new relationships among themselves. This calls not only for knowledge and skill on their part but also for the slow growth of those intangible assets, mutual trust and acceptance of new habits of co-operation.[1]

Argentina today can be described as an economic enigma — a basically resourceful country that has undergone a period of economic stagnation during a decade of almost unprecedented economic expansion throughout most of the world, a country making a serious but largely unsuccessful attempt to take the road of steady economic growth.

After the fall of Perón's military dictatorship in 1955, Argentine and foreign experts, in their search for possible explanations for the nation's economic collapse, assumed that the barriers to growth were fundamentally of an *economic* character and that the problem of Argentina's development could be adequately dealt with by economic measures alone. Following their advice, several steps were taken by post-1955 governments to solve crucial economic problems, such as Argentina's

[1] International Labour Office: *Report of the Director-General*, Report I, Part I, International Labour Conference, Forty-third Session (Geneva, 1959), pp. 51–52.

I

ability to attract foreign capital, the intensive exploitation of the country's natural resources, and the necessity of balancing the nation's trade position over the long run. Furthermore, the Frondizi administration seems to regard massive industrialization as the remedy for all illnesses which have plagued the country since the mid-1940's.

Of course, economic factors play an important role in determining whether or not economic development occurs, and the rate of growth of an economy. But Argentina's experience between 1945 and 1955 and its failure to recover, despite basically sound economic measures taken since then, suggest that something of more vital importance lies behind the troubles besetting the nation's economy. The country still enjoys a very high standard of living — certainly one of the highest among the so-called "underdeveloped" countries. Argentina provides a market big enough to permit the emergence of a highly diversified industry. The nation's grasslands (the "pampas") are among the world's richest agricultural and pastoral areas. Lack of capital may have been a problem during the Perón era, but before and after the dictatorship, foreign capital has consistently filled the gap left by a periodically insufficient, but usually adequate, rate of domestic capital formation.[2] Argentina's labor force is certainly adaptable, skillful, and alert; and the middle sectors of the Argentine society have never lacked in entrepreneurship. The nation has adequate access to foreign technical knowledge and advances, and its entrepreneurs have demonstrated in the past that they are endowed with a degree of technical competence suitable for industrial growth. Why, then, economic stagnation? Why the failure to recover? Why the appearance and popular support of demagogues? Why ill-conceived economic policies, dictatorship, and pernicious state intervention in all sectors of the nation's life?

Since World War II, there has been increasing awareness of the fact that *social* and *cultural* barriers may be as important as economic factors in determining whether economic growth will occur in a given society. As yet, however, governments throughout the free world have largely failed to apply the newly gained knowledge of social processes in economic development as an implementation of economic policies in their own countries. Argentina is no exception to the rule. Little has been done by the Argentine government or other institutions or groups within the society to face the problem of the nation's economic development realistically from a social point of view. This situation is of particular importance because, as we shall seek to demonstrate in this book, the nature of Argentina's basic problem is fundamentally, al-

[2] See United Nations, C.E.P.A.L., *El Desarrollo Económico de la Argentina*, Part I (Mexico, 1959), pp. 27–36.

though not exclusively, *social* rather than economic. Therefore, unless the Argentine society develops into an organism consistent with the essential requirements of economic development (*i.e.,* a continuous rise in per capita output in the long run and the balanced distribution of the steadily rising national income among all sectors of the population), the economy is very likely to follow a slow, discontinuous, and eventually a static course.

An analysis of the Argentine "national character," based on a study of the value-orientation profile of the Argentine society, will demonstrate that some cultural traits of the bulk of the population are inimical to the emergence of social relationships which would enable individuals to act concertedly in the pursuit of common goals and interests. This feature, *i.e.,* the fact that Argentines are a "conglomeration" of people rather than an organic "community," together with the fact that those same cultural traits also constitute a powerful barrier to the appearance of "Western-capitalistic-like" economic initiative in the bulk of the society's members, is and has been in the past a fundamental impediment retarding the nation's economic growth. Of course, it would be unrealistic to assume that one element *alone* is the cause of Argentina's economic stagnation. The viewpoint taken in this book is that the basically passive, apathetic value-orientation profile of the Argentine society must be regarded as the *critical* factor limiting the possibilities of steady, long-run economic development.

Based on a brief study of the need structure and personality formation of Argentina's population, we shall also suggest that this society is basically static with respect to changes in the value orientations of its members. Therefore, unless the incoherent forces within today's society are somehow reconciled, the nation's development will continue to be a succession of ups and downs, depending on which leader brings what force at what time to the dominant position in society. In the future, economic measures may indeed foster economic development for a certain period, the duration of which is, for our purposes, irrelevant. But unless a development of the society's value-orientation profile towards higher degrees of activity is simultaneously fostered, most economic gains achieved during one period may be wiped out in a following one by social or political dislocations. In other words, steady economic development cannot take place without a progressive and radical socio-cultural transformation.

Obviously, this transformation cannot be brought about by the conscious and deliberate choice of the bulk of the Argentine population. Regardless of the social layer to which they belong, the problem is precisely that Argentines are unable to co-operate in the furtherance of their common interest. We contend, however, that there exists an area where, because of the future industrial course which the Argentine economy must take if the economy is to progress, a process of gradual social change may be initiated with a minimum of interference by a minority of responsible leaders within the society. The area is that of industrial relations. We shall assert that the solution to Argentina's basic problem (from an economic-development standpoint) can be reached by a new approach to industrial relations. It is through the creation of a "new" industrial environment that a gradual, long-run transformation of the value-orientation profile of the Argentine society can be achieved.

2 THE ARGENTINE NATIONAL CHARACTER

T HE PRIMARY aim of this chapter is to identify and analyze those cultural traits of the Argentine people which are the reasons for the apparent failure of the Argentine society to develop into an organic "community." The development of such a "community spirit" is an indispensable condition that would make co-operation possible at all levels of the nation's life and thus contribute to Argentina's economic growth.

THEORY AND ASSUMPTIONS

The analysis of the Argentine national character as presented in this chapter follows the concept of "basic personality" developed by Dr. Abram Kardiner and Dr. Ralph Linton. In his introduction to Dr. Kardiner's *The Psychological Frontiers of Society,* Linton states that the concept of "basic personality" rests upon the following postulates:

1. That the individual's early experiences exert a lasting effect upon his personality, especially upon the development of his projective systems.

2. That similar experiences will tend to produce similar personality configurations in the individuals who are subjected to them.

3. That the techniques which the members of any society employ in the care and rearing of children are culturally patterned and will tend to be similar, although never identical, for various families within the society.

4. That the culturally patterned techniques for the care and rearing of children differ from one society to another.

If these postulates are correct, and they seem to be supported by a wealth of evidence, it follows:

1. That the members of any given society will have many elements of early experience in common.

2. That as a result of this they will have many elements of personality in common.

3. That since the early experience of individuals differs from one society to another, the personality norms for various societies will also differ.

5

The *basic personality type* for any society is that personality configuration which is shared by the bulk of the society's members as a result of the early experiences which they have in common.[1]

This does not mean that the behavior patterns of the bulk of the society's members will be equal or even similar. An individual's overt behavior is determined by his personality characteristics together with all environmental stimuli which he faces. Thus there is a wide range of differences in the verbalized attitudes and behavior patterns of whole groups of persons within every society, of the particular society's individual members, and even of the same individual when he is playing different roles. Indeed, an individual's overt behavior may appear to the casual observer to be in complete contradiction to the basic nature of his personality. What Linton calls the "basic personality type"

> does not correspond to the total personality of the individual but rather to the projective system or, in different phraseology, the value attitude systems which are basic to the individual's personality configuration. Thus the same basic personality type may be reflected in many different forms of behavior and may enter into many different total personality configurations.[2]

These "value attitude systems" will be called in our exposition (*dominant*) *value orientations,* following Dr. Florence R. Kluckhohn's terminology. We thus define a society's basic personality type (which determines the so-called "national character") by defining those (dominant) value orientations shared by the bulk of the society's members as a result of the early experiences which they have had in common. Kluckhohn has called this pattern of dominant value orientations the *value-orientation profile* of a society.[3]

Kluckhohn bases her conceptual scheme upon the following two fundamental assumptions:

> *There is a limited number of basic human problems for which all peoples at all times and in all places must find some solution.* The five common human problems tentatively singled out as those of key importance can be stated in the form of questions:

[1] Kardiner, A., *et al.: The Psychological Frontiers of Society* (New York, Columbia University Press, 1945), pp. vii–viii. (Italics in the original.)

[2] *Ibid.,* p. viii.

[3] Kluckhohn, F., "Dominant and Variant Value Orientations," in Kluckhohn, Murray, and Schneider, eds.: *Personality in Nature, Society and Culture,* 2nd. ed., rev. and enl. (New York, Alfred A. Knopf, 1955), Ch. 21, pp. 342–357. Our definition of a society's basic personality type does not exclude the presence of individuals or whole groups of individuals within the society whose personalities are defined by other, *variant* value orientations. Indeed, variant value orientations are not only permitted but actually required to insure the maintenance of the society (*ibid.,* esp. p. 352). In our discussion of the Argentine people, however, we will only describe *dominant* value orientations, which will be simply referred to as "value orientations."

(1) What are the *innate predispositions* of man? (Basic human nature)

(2) What is the relation of *man to nature?*

(3) What is the significant *time dimension?*

(4) What is the valued *personality type?*

(5) What is the dominant modality of the *relationship of man to other men?*

The problems as stated in these questions are regarded as constant; they arise inevitably out of the human situation. The solutions found for them are variable but not limitlessly so. It is the second major assumption of the conceptual scheme that the *variability in solutions is variability within a range of possible solutions.*[4]

The value-orientation profile of the Argentine society will be analyzed following Kluckhohn's framework of type solutions to the above-mentioned five basic human problems.[5]

An individual's personality will be assumed to be defined by two elements: his *value orientations* and his *need structure.* No claim is made that this simplified scheme is sufficient to comprehend all of an individual's personality. Many other elements could be added: his intelligence, his energy, his creativity, his preferences, and that part of his cognitive image of the world which is not included in our definition of value orientations, among others. But we consider our scheme adequate to shape a consistent, although overly simplified, model by means of which some characteristics of today's Argentine society and the external behavior of the nation's population can be logically accounted for. On the other hand, in defining an individual's personality it is necessary to specify both his need structure and value orientations, since there is nothing in the nature of personality which causes certain needs and certain value orientations to be *necessarily* associated with each other. In the process of personality formation, needs which have been acquired help to determine value orientations, and acquired value orientations help to determine needs. At any given point in time in a society — for instance, given a particular social structure, physical environment, and technical knowledge — an individual with a certain need structure may be likely to have certain value orientations. But at another point in time, under different external conditions, the same needs may be associated with other value orientations.[6]

---

[4] *Ibid.*, p. 346. (Italics in the original.)

[5] For the complete framework of type solutions, see *ibid.*, p. 346.

[6] See Hagen, E. E.: *How Economic Growth Begins: A Study in the Theory of Social Change* (Massachusetts Institute of Technology, 1959–60, mimeographed manuscript), Chapter IV. Our model follows closely Professor Hagen's discussion of personality, although the element of "world view" in Professor Hagen's scheme has been substituted for by Dr. Kluckhohn's "value orientations" as a further simplification. Both concepts overlap to some extent, but Professor Hagen's is unquestionably of broader scope.

It may be necessary to state clearly that by assuming that an Argentine "national character" indeed exists, based on the premise that basic personality types tend to differ between various societies, we automatically imply that there are no differences in the *basic personality structure* of members of different social layers. In other words, members of different social sectors share, by assumption, similar value orientations.

Dominant Value Orientations

Basic Human Nature

There is some evidence that the Argentine views human nature as a Mixture of Good and Bad, although easily corruptible. The Argentine parent thinks that children are naturally rebellious and lazy. Although children are often spanked, punishments are often considered to be insufficient to set them on the desired road. A child (or a youth, for that matter) is always in great danger of being "badly influenced" by other children, so special precautions must be taken to protect the child from pernicious friendships. The same is true of a sister or wife. As anywhere else in Latin America, a wife

> . . . should be sheltered from the temptations of this mundane world and protected from any dangers — particularly from men outside the family — that might threaten her virtue. The woman's place is the home, raising and tending children, dedicated to the domestic arts, and setting a noble example for her husband who is considered of lesser moral stature.[7]

Although, as will be seen later, there is more to this attitude towards a wife than mere doubts of her innate predispositions, the view of human nature as easily corruptible certainly helps to give shape to the great precautions an Argentine husband takes to shelter his wife from dangerous influences.

Corruption in government and public administrative offices, although often criticized, is taken for granted. Whether an officeholder takes bribes or not, Argentines assume that he does. Consequently, officeholders will usually take bribes whenever they think they can get away with it. Indeed, there is abundant evidence that bribery is a common feature of Argentine public administrative offices.

These commentaries would tend to suggest that the Argentine views his neighbor's human nature as essentially Bad. Neighbors and, to some extent, friends are indeed considered to be potentially dangerous (and

[7] Whyte, W. F., and Holmberg, A. R.: *Human Problems of U. S. Enterprise in Latin America, 1956* (Ithaca, N. Y., New York State School of Industrial and Labor Relations, Cornell University), p. 5.

potentially costly) mainly because almost everybody is expected to envy his neighbor's prosperity and wish him harm. Towards those who are not of the family or intimate friends, the reasonable attitude is suspicion. On this subject, José Ortega y Gasset makes the following comment:

> There is a relative justification to the defensiveness of the Argentine. His wealth, social position, or public office of any rank are in constant danger due to the pressure of appetites surrounding them, unchecked by any other rule. Where impudence is the common trait of social relations, it is necessary to be perpetually on the alert.[8]

On the other hand, when an individual's misdemeanor is uncovered, when a loved one does wrong and is therefore punished, he is considered to have had "bad luck." In the Argentine folklore the *gaucho,* the epic symbol of Argentina's heroic past, never "kills"; "mishaps" occur to him "while fighting. . . ." According to *criollo* ethics, writes the poet Jorge Luis Borges,

> the spilling of blood is not especially memorable. . . . One afternoon I heard an old man gently grumble "In my day, who was there who hadn't a death to his account?" Nor shall I forget the uncouth fellow who said to me gravely: "Señor Borges, I may have been in prison many times; but always for homicide." [9]

One who suffers punishment feels unfortunate. Since conduct is believed to be formed by influences that play upon the individual, he may feel that he has been stupid or that he has listened to the wrong advice. Or he will blame "bad luck" or somebody else for his misfortune. Above all, he feels *ashamed* for having been caught or fooled. But it would never occur to him that he is, by nature, Bad or Evil; he feels little guilt.[10] An impulse to do wrong is resisted mainly because the individual fears the law or public opinion — "el qué diran" (the-what-will-they-say) — not because he is led to do right by his conscience or by standards of conduct learned through education. Furthermore, whether Good or Bad, an individual is only perfectible through charity and devotion, never by means of his work, enterprise, or material achievements.

---

[8] Ortega y Gasset, J.: "Intimidades," in *Obras Completas,* 3rd. ed., 2 vols. (Madrid, Espasa-Calpe S.A., 1943), p. 670. Unless otherwise specified, all translations from Spanish into English appearing in this book are by the author.

[9] As quoted in Pendle, G.: *Argentina* (London, Oxford University Press, 1955), p. 133.

[10] Gerhard Piers and Milton B. Singer develop the concepts of "shame" and "guilt" cultures in *Shame and Guilt* (Springfield, Ill., Charles C. Thomas, 1953). We suggest that in the Argentine society shame is more important relative to guilt than in Anglo-American culture, although less so than in Japanese or American Indian cultures. See also Hagen, E. E.: *op. cit.,* Chapter VII.

These traits help to explain why individuals or whole groups of people tend to blame other individuals or groups for failures or short-comings to which they themselves have clearly contributed. An example can be found in the field of industrial relations. Argentine industry is presently plagued by the day-to-day deepening of the cleavage separat-ing government, management, and labor. Each party blames the other two for all political, social, and economic difficulties the country is undergoing, and at the same time each party expects the other two to solve the problem (this applies mainly to labor and management, al-though it is to some extent true of Argentine governments since 1955). As a consequence, there is little initiative, little co-operation, and little vigor in industry. Under current circumstances, this constitutes by itself a formidable barrier to economic development.

Man's Relation to Nature

The Argentine illustrates Kluckhohn's Man Subjugated to Na-ture position. He simply accepts the inevitable as the inevitable.

> Raúl Scalabrini Ortiz has described the *porteño* [the inhabitant of Buenos Aires] as *el hombre que está solo y espera*, "the man who is alone, and waits" — or it may be "hopes," for the Spanish verb *esperar* means both "to hope" and "to wait." The Argentines, even while they possess unfounded faith in their country's future, are aware of their geographical remote-ness. . . .
>
> As for the man of the "camp," he too inhabits a lonely world. The pampa is so huge and so empty. . . .[11]

Ortega y Gasset suggests that the Argentine pampa (*i.e.,* Nature) has shaped the personality of its inhabitants.The pampa's never-ending hori-zon and its miraculous fertility promise an inexhaustible source of plenty. "The pampa promises, promises, promises. . . ." In it

> everything lives in the distance — and from the distance. Nobody is where he is, but in front of himself, far ahead, in his individual horizon, from where he governs and executes his real, present, and effective life. The Ar-gentine lives what I would call his *individual concrete future*. This is not the shared future of a common ideal, of a collective Utopia; each individual lives *his own illusions* as if they had already come true. . . .
>
> The sole vocation of the typical Argentine is to be now what he believes he is already. Therefore, he devotes himself not to a reality, but to an image. But one can only devote oneself to an image by contemplating it.[12]

The Argentine watches the world around him pass by. He waits and hopes, uncommitted in his solitude. Writes James Bruce:

[11] Pendle, G., *op. cit.,* p. 133. (Italics in the original.)
[12] Ortega y Gasset, J.: *op. cit.,* pp. 657 and 677. (Italics in the original.)

Argentines want most to live peacefully. They seek a tranquil existence, hence are willing to talk but go along rather than fight back . . . even among those Argentines who are excitable and passionate in other ways, the desire to keep out of trouble, to remain uninvolved, to refuse to upset oneself unduly, is traditional.[18]

But although Argentines view the world around them with passivity, although poetry and music (both urban and folk) almost invariably express disillusion, nostalgia, melancholy, and frustration, Argentines are not fatalists. They have complete faith in themselves and in Argentina's future and destiny:

> The Argentine people are not content to be one nation among many; they require an exalted destiny, they demand of themselves a proud future, they have no taste for a history without triumph and are determined to command.[14]

But they wait, and hope, and expect the attainment of the promised future *not by their own effort* but by "magic," or divine grace. Eduardo Mallea mentions that the Argentine motto is "God will provide." [15] We have often heard Argentines say "God is Argentine," thus there is nothing to worry about. This leads us into a discussion of religious feelings in Argentina.

Women are the pillars of the Church. It is around the mother that the Argentine family performs its religious duties. Consequently, men look upon religion as largely a woman's business and play little part in it unless encouraged or constrained to do so. Men even boast of being angrily anticlerical. However, anticlericalism (if at all sincere) is not necessarily the outcome of a loss of religious faith. Such boasts may go hand in hand with faith in the powers of Jesus, the patron saints, and the Blessed Virgin. But the priest is thought to be a somewhat self-interested obstacle to the private relationship between oneself and God. A definition of this relationship, however, is carefully (although unconsciously) avoided. God exists, no doubt, and one should pay Him respect. But God is not easily accessible despite man's good intentions. God is like luck, since an individual's effort, ability, and initiative count little if He does not help. A favorite saint or the Blessed Virgin, however, is believed to be more accessible and predictable, more able and willing to afford protection in certain matters. Similarly, the distinction between God and Jesus is usually blurred or nonexistent. This approach to religion can be explained in terms of *personalismo:*

[18] Bruce, James: *Those Perplexing Argentines* (New York, Longmans, Green & Co., 1953), p. 34.
[14] Ortega y Gasset, J.: *op. cit.,* p. 633; as quoted in Hanke, L.: *South America* (Princeton, N. J., D. Van Nostrand Co., 1959), p. 151.
[15] In *Historia de una Pasión Argentina* (Buenos Aires, Espasa-Calpe, 1945), p. 20.

Almost everyone who has written about the cultures of Latin America has called attention to a phenomenon called personalism, a characteristic, which, like the outlook on the structure of society, was inherited from the mother country of Spain. In a sense, personalism may be regarded as a variety of individualism, but it is not the same kind of individualism that is either practised or preached here in the United States. In Latin America it is more than the doctrine that the individual, and not society, is of paramount importance in human life. Personalism goes even deeper than this. Not man in the abstract, but man in the concrete, becomes the center of the universe. And the concrete man in the center of the universe is the person himself. . . .

In the realm of ideology and religion we see manifestations of [this] phenomenon. For most Latin Americans, . . . God is a kind of vague entity like a corporation. He is a hazy and inaccessible power with whom it is impossible to deal directly. Consequently, He gets little attention in religious life. The same is not true of the saints, however. They act as intermediaries between God and man and are viewed as real people with whom it is possible to personalize relations . . . in religious life one frequently identifies his fortunes in life with a particular saint, just as in politics one may do so with a particular political leader.[16]

We suggest that all these personality traits are different forms of an acute feeling of *impotence* in controlling the forces of Nature. The forces behind events appear to Argentines not only unmanageable, but also unpredictable, random. Thus, Argentines are very fond of gambling. Most see in a lucky turn of the wheels of fortune not only the easiest, but also the sole, means by which their dream of wealth and plenty may one day come true. Large amounts of money, sometimes well beyond their financial means, are bet weekly in horse races, the lottery, cards, and *quiniela* (the illegal numbers racket). We suggest that although gambling does not establish order and predictability in the Argentine's world, it relieves him at least momentarily of his anxiety of being impotent against an unknown external force. Gambling "personalizes" this force in a deck of cards, a horse, or the lottery number.

In summary, then, great success is obtained by waiting, by hoping, by the favor of the saints, or by luck — not primarily by thrift, work, and enterprise. This idea has certainly a negative effect on economic initiative and the Argentine's political philosophy. And it obviously checks an individual's drive for social organization. Where everything depends upon the inevitability of future events, upon luck, or upon divine intervention, *there is no need for active community enterprise.* The individual, like an

---

[16] Whyte, W., and Holmberg, A.: *op. cit.,* p. 3. It should be noted that the idea of "man in the concrete" as the "center of the universe" is also a consequence of the *Being-orientation* and the *"need dependency"* of the society's members.

institution or like the community, may hope, pray, work, or fight. But he is not likely ever to be the architect of his own destiny.

Time Dimension

Argentines emphasize Present time. There is no doubt that they pay high respect to their traditions and historical past. They are proud of their heroes and wars of independence; their literature and folklore clearly show the existence of a certain nostalgia for earlier times, for the *gaucho,* for the old heroic Argentina; but the traditions of the past are considered just what they are: traditions, something to be proud of, but not something to be maintained or recaptured.

On the other hand, as has already been mentioned, the Argentine has "a blind faith in the glorious destiny of his nation . . ." but he does not *live or work for* the future; *he contemplates its image,*

> he considers all the future grandeurs already accomplished, and feeling himself a part of them, he appropriates to his own person the glory of this collective future as if it were a *present* reality.[17]

The future may be bright, but the ways and means by which it is to be accomplished are most uncertain and unpredictable. In fact, "the man of Buenos Aires, in his solitude, is bewildered when he attempts to imagine what are the characteristics of the nation that he and his compatriots are forging." [18]

There is some reason to believe that this cultural attachment to the Present and this emphasis on immediate goals have been accentuated over the last decades. The writings and works of the nineteenth-century men who shaped the union of the provinces, the 1853 Constitution, and the political framework of modern Argentina show that they were leaders with some sense of future, long-run objectives. Their methods and political approach may be questioned, but they were certainly men who acted according to principle and reason rather than self-interest and emotion. Nineteenth-century Argentina was a young country, full of vitality, where everything — the building of the cities, a political system, an organized economy — was still to be done. Early immigration waves brought to Argentine shores people driven mainly by their pioneer spirit who were prepared to make sacrifices so that their descendants might have a degree of well-being to which they could not aspire in their country of origin. Nowadays immigrants are impelled by the hope of immediate gains. People no longer emigrate for the sake of their descendants; they emigrate primarily for their own

---

[17] Ortega y Gasset, J.: *op. cit.,* as quoted in Hanke, L.: *op. cit.,* p. 152. (Italics added.)
[18] Pendle, G.: *op. cit.,* p. 133.

sakes. The pioneer spirit has largely disappeared, giving way to a mercenary outlook. But, what is more important, when they land at Buenos Aires they find themselves among apathetic, contented people who have replaced the high ideals and ambitions traditional in previous generations with a new, passive outlook — "God will provide."

The social and economic implications for a society whose members emphasize Present time are fairly obvious. Such an emphasis is inimical to conscientious planning for the future; to long-run economic, political, or social commitments; to the emergence of a collective sense of duty — especially of the sense of duty to do productive work; or to furthering the interest of, or unselfishly co-operating with, a group, an organization, or a community, except as it is to the short-run or at least easily foreseeable advantage of the individual to do so.

Valued Personality Type

Expressed in Kluckhohn's terms, the Argentine's orientation is essentially Being, though with certain Being-in-Becoming overtones.

> The essence of the Being orientation is that it stresses the spontaneous expression of what is considered to be "given" in the personality. The orientation is . . . essentially *non*-developmental. . . . The Being-in-Becoming orientation shares with the Being a great concern with what the human being *is* rather than what he can *accomplish,* but here the similarity ends. . . . The Being-in-Becoming orientation emphasizes *self*-realization — *self*-development — of all aspects of the self as an integrated whole.[19]

The emphasis on Being starts in the concept of *argentinidad* (literally, "argentinity") itself. "To be from the Argentine nation, to be of this people, this is a reason for elemental, irrefutable, and axiomatic pride for any true Argentine. . . ."[20]

> Argentines refuse to accept any truth which makes them inferior to anyone else. . . . perhaps it is this overwhelming pride of the Argentines that leads them to believe that they can live aloof from any interdependence of nations . . . and that they need have no fear of whatever changes may come.[21]

Argentines have a high opinion of their own worth as a people; and even in the most trivial matters, admiration and respect are paid to everything which is assumed to be born with the individual: his sagacity, his courage, his artistic talents, his manliness, his "innate" ability to play *futbol* (soccer)! Any derogatory reference to what a person *is*, is taken

---

[19] Kluckhohn, F.: *op. cit.,* p. 350. (Italics in the original.)
[20] Ortega y Gasset, J.: *op. cit.,* p. 676, as quoted in Hanke, L.: *op. cit.,* p. 152.
[21] President Marcelo T. de Alvear, as quoted by Bruce, J.: *op. cit.,* p. 7.

as the most serious affront, as an insult to the dignity (*la dignidad*) of the individual in question. "This desire to assert one's self, to achieve self-respect," writes Bruce, "extends from the poorest Argentine news vendor to the highest official in the land, and it affects every phase of Argentine life." [22]

Manliness is a virtue. And the quintessence of manliness is fearlessness, physical strength, pride, and readiness to defend one's own honor and that of one's family and closest friends — briefly, to Be a *macho* (male). Manliness is directly ascribed to its physical origin, and the language used to refer to it is frankly physiological. Such a concept of manhood drives the Argentine to justify his virility by means of repeated demonstrations of sexual prowess. Success with women is thus a powerful gratification to the Argentine's self-esteem. The *conquistador* (women's conqueror) — strong and irresistible, sung in prose and verse — has always been a model and a goal for young generations of Argentines. This drive for justification of manhood tends to outweigh the moral precepts which he has learned, and gives rise to a curious double standard: while a mother, a wife, or a sister is considered to be pure and holy and is to be sheltered from the temptations of this mundane life, women outside the family or immediate social group are regarded as fair game for every man, something to be enjoyed if the opportunity arises. For our purposes, the relevance of the *macho* complex is that it constitutes, not a drive to solve problems to prove oneself, but a drive to be a male and to defend one's honor to prove it. It is part of a value orientation which compels the Argentine to "Be" something rather than to "Do" or "Accomplish" something. [23]

Another expression of this Being-orientation is the reluctance to accord *social* status to individuals who are *only economically* in a power position. This feature might be explained as a belief in all men's equality before God, or in the ultimate futility of earthly life, or as a lack of faith in man's ability to control his own destiny. Being indeed congruent with the total set of value orientations of the Argentine, some weight should be certainly given to these partial explanations. In our opinion, however, this feature is fundamentally a consequence of the respect the Argentine pays to human personality rather than to human rights, possessions, and accomplishments. Values relating to money, for instance, are generally not those of Protestant capitalism. The possession of money is not by itself honorable or a basis for social recognition. In fact, only very recently have income and wealth been reluctantly accepted as ele-

[22] *Ibid.*, p. 22.
[23] These topics are further discussed in Whyte, W., and Holmberg, A.: *op. cit.*, pp. 5 and 6; and in Hagen, E. E.: *op. cit.*, Chapter VII.

ments to be added to education, religion, conduct, way of life, occupation, family background, and prejudices as determinants of social status. Morally, money is neutral. Even the way in which it is acquired is in itself not subject to serious moral judgment. It is the way in which it is spent that counts. (One typical example: Everybody in Argentina knew and could see that Perón and especially his wife amassed their immense fortune by — to say the least — most devious means. The masses, however, never indicted them on this account, obviously because they spent — indeed a very small — part of their wealth in helping the poor and needy.) Money confers prestige and social standing only if spent in a morally sanctioned manner. The landed aristocracy have tended to regard paternalistic practices as the proper way of using their wealth. Indeed, many of them have always exhibited a suitable sense of responsibility for the material well-being of their workers. Such a *patrón* usually acquires great prestige within the orbit of his influence, thereby escaping the contemptuous opinion his subordinates may have of rich people in general.

On the other hand, not to attach *moral* value to money does not mean that money is despised. On the contrary, money is eagerly sought by Argentines for two main reasons. The first is that since money properly spent may permit one to gain (or "buy") social prestige, money is regarded as something that enables a man to be what he most desires. In a sense, it gives him the power to choose between being good and being evil. Secondly, money has an additional strong appeal: it enables people to avoid the vicissitudes of daily work.

In Argentina, as in most of Latin America, work is not a particularly esteemed or dignifying activity.

[Work] is nothing in itself to be rewarded for. It is rather a necessary burden that must be borne by some people as part of the pattern of living. . . . It is the nature of things that some are born to leisure and others are born to work, even though the latter may not be particularly happy with their lot nor value the work activities they perform. Thus on the part of socially mobile people, who were not fortunate enough to be born to the leisure class, there is . . . a tendency to avoid the stigma of manual labor, for it identifies one with the lower class. A true gentleman, if he works at all, works only with his mind. He regards it as undignified to dirty his hands on anything that is identified with physical labor.[24]

This contempt for manual work as well as, generally, the emphasis on Being, which has been described in earlier paragraphs, must have appeared first in members of the landowning class, who still constitute

[24] Whyte, W., and Holmberg, A.: *op. cit.,* p. 9. The discussion that follows is based on concepts expounded by Professor E. E. Hagen: *op. cit.,* Chapter VII.

the nucleus of the Argentine aristocracy. Historically, the power of the aristocracy has rested on their control over land (the main source of income) and over people (*peones*). Except for the initial generations, who took their lands *de facto,* the position that gave power to the aristocracy was typically inherited and only to a small degree achieved. No man in any society can live without the feeling that he has worth. Since the most important factor giving members of the landowning class their status was birth, it was therefore impossible for them to feel that they were the same sort of persons as "the masses," the position to which they were born being merely an accident. Since they had no superior achievement to justify a sense of individual worth, it was essential for them to feel that *innately* they were different from, and more elevated individuals than, the uncivilized masses. For the same reasons, the aristocratic élite had *necessarily* to find all elements of the life-pattern of the middle or low sectors of the population unworthy. Thus they looked down — and continue to do so — upon manual work, industry, trading, and to some extent money — especially since their loss of economic power to the rising middle sectors of the population. On the other hand, the sources of aristocratic status were enhanced: landownership, family name, ancestry, education, and to a minor extent intellectual and artistic work.

It is a recognized fact that lower social strata tend to attach high prestige to all those values and life-patterns which they identify with higher-status groups. This attitude must have constituted the main mechanism through which the masses developed their distaste for manual work and their reluctance to accord superior status to individuals on the basis of economic power and achievements alone. Most importantly (from an economic-development point of view), through this mechanism the Argentine society as a whole has developed an orientation which still causes it to attach higher prestige to the landowner than to businessmen, to stock raising and agriculture than to industry.

But there is more to the Argentines' scale of values. As a consequence of the cultural characteristics we have just expounded, when for some reason a member of the aristocracy decides or is forced to earn his living away from the traditional landowning pattern, he turns to the professions rather than to business. Furthermore, at college he typically chooses a field other than physical sciences and engineering. Or if for one reason or another he turns to the physical sciences, he will typically select a "pure" field, with little or no technical application. Consequently, members of lower sectors in the social ladder have closely followed this pattern of preferences and conferred occupational prestige according to the same order. In other words, when the average Argentine chooses to develop beyond the status he has acquired by birth (and there is evidence that this phenomenon is not uncommon, especially within the middle sectors), he will usually try to do so, not by developing his manual skills or by accomplishing business or industrial feats, but by developing his *intellectual* skills. He will follow an academic career typically in a field which is not "directly productive" from an economic point of view—medicine, law, social sciences, etc. An analysis of Argentine higher-education figures and their comparison with those of economically highly developed countries and others in process of industrialization (Table I) show these tendencies. The prestige which Argentines confer on members of the professions as against "nonprofessionals" is noticeable: one addresses oneself deferentially to an academic graduate by mentioning his title—*Arquitecto, Ingeniero,* or *Escribano,* for instance.

TABLE I

Enrollment in Institutions of Higher Education in Argentina
and Other Selected Countries

			PERCENTAGE ENROLLED IN		
Country	Year	Enrollment per 100,000 of National Population	Law and Medical Sciences	Engineering and Agricultural Sciences	Others[a]
Argentina	1954	756	56	19	25
Brazil	1954	117	54	14	32
France	1954	416	43	6	51
Germany (Fed. Rep.)	1954	282	41	21	38
India	1953	147	7	4	89
Japan	1954	686 (1955)	18	16	66
United States	1954	1,816 (1955)	6	10	84

[a] Including social, natural, and physical sciences; humanities; economics; commerce and business; etc.

SOURCE: United Nations: *Report on the World Social Situation* (New York, 1957), pp. 75-85.

That the Argentines' Being-orientation is inimical to the nation's industrial — and thus economic — development should be fairly obvious by now. However, one point should be particularly stressed. It refers to the effect of this value orientation on the authority relationship between a superior and a subordinate in an industrial or administrative situation.[25]

We have already mentioned *personalismo* as a cultural characteristic of the Argentine. This feature, however, is only one blade of the scissors.

[25] Obviously, the following commentaries apply to all conceivable situations in which a relationship of authority exists. Argentine students, for instance, must be strictly — we would say "militarily" — obedient to teachers.

The other is the reluctance of the individual occupying a position of power or prestige to delegate authority. And both characteristics are the direct result of the emphasis being placed on Being. In the industrial or administrative situation, for instance, these complementary cultural traits manifest themselves in two ways. First, as a result of an emphasis on Being rather than on Doing or Accomplishing, prime stress is placed on, and respect is accorded to, the *person* who occupies the office or holds a job or position rather than on the office or position itself; in the same vein, a business or factory tends to be identified with its owner or owning family rather than viewed as a collective, impersonal organization. Second, and conversely, since it is not the job or office that is the object of respect and value but the person who occupies it, and since, having reached a higher position, his value orientations lead him to assume that he *Is* superior to his subordinates, the individual in a position of authority will not be likely to have self-doubts regarding the justification of such authority. He will tend to be more or less autocratic. Furthermore, since subordinates *Are* inferior, and thus not to be trusted in the performance of their functions, and since any failure or inadequacy in the socially acceptable performance of his job will reflect *personally* upon himself and his family, he will naturally be reluctant to delegate his authority and responsibilities.

On the other hand, the subordinate will probably not dare to challenge directly, in a face-to-face situation, the authority of an individual who *Is* superior to himself. This, however, does not mean that he will be content with his superior's actions and orders or that his anxiety will be thereby mitigated. On the contrary, he will tend to suppress his rising anxiety and rage (which leads to apathy through undue consumption of energy in handling his inner conflicts), or he will discharge them in sanctioned ways on sanctioned targets: *his subordinates* or, at home, his children. Furthermore, in due course he may indeed retaliate *indirectly* against his superior by assuming negative rules of conduct at work or by embracing "popularly sanctioned" creeds which promise him the recognition he has been denied in his job.

We are here touching upon the crux of the Argentine industrial relations problem. In our opinion, this is one of the most difficult cultural barriers which will have to be overcome if industry is to play the dynamic role necessary to make steady economic development possible. More will be said about it in following chapters.

Finally, since office- or job-holders do not derive status specifically from their position, they will feel no identification with their jobs (and with the purposes of the organization) and thus will tend not to work any harder than is necessary to keep their places or to earn promotion. Indeed, the Argentine thinks of advancing himself in order that he may pass the burden of petty work to others; to many people, success means reaching a point in an organization where they no longer have to work or where they can come and go as they please. Similarly, it is not unusual to find professionals or educated people lacking any sense of mission or calling. It is not uncommon for teachers or even high-school and university professors to take little interest in their classes and students or to call strikes in demand for higher salaries. And very recently Argentine physicians were involved in a long and costly strike, too. In both cases, there are other factors underlying such attitudes which must be taken into consideration and cannot be discussed here. But it seems obvious that if the sense of mission or calling which is normally expected of teachers and members of the medical profession indeed existed, it would far outweigh other material or personal considerations. José Ortega y Gasset writes that the Argentine is:

> a marvellously gifted man . . . who has never devoted himself to the activity he carries out, who has never accepted it as his vital goal, who never considers it to be definitive but rather a transitory stage in the way to his ideal: advancement in wealth and social status.
>
> . . . I think that professional vocations are rare beyond measure in Argentina or, conversely, that the typical Argentine does not abandon himself, spontaneously, to any particular occupation. Not even to leisure.[26]

Similarly, only rarely will competence or training outweigh other, personal ("Being") considerations in the appointment of public administrative officers or in the recruitment of managerial cadres in industry, business, or social organizations (unions, for instance). Therefore, it is only understandable that those individuals who do have special training or competence will tend to use it as a weapon against others for private advantage rather than as a personal contribution to the common welfare and progress.

Modality of Relationship

In Argentina, the dominant modality of relationship of man to other men is Lineal; in other words, the family, and its continuity through time, plays an extremely significant role in the patterning of human relations.

Without any doubt, descent and family name are still the most distinguishing mark of an individual in Argentina. An Argentine uses both his father's and his mother's family name. And an Argentine wife uses on

[26] Ortega y Gasset, J.: *op. cit.*, pp. 671 and 674.

all occasions both her maiden and her husband's family name. This is all in accord with Spanish tradition. But elsewhere in Latin America family names are rarely given such a paramount importance as in Argentina. A family name serves several purposes: one can locate easily the ethnic background of its bearer, his political ideology, economic position, social status, descent and kinship, friends, and religion. But, above all, a family name is a source of pride for every true Argentine, rich or poor, member of the aristocracy or of a lower social layer.

In general, the extended type of family organization has been somewhat broken down in recent decades, owing to an increase in geographical mobility and the growth of urbanism, but in rural areas it is still not uncommon to find a considerable number of relatives sharing a household with a patriarch and his direct descendants, and even in urban areas, close contact is always maintained with kin outside of the immediate family. This feature in itself would not be harmful to the subsistence of the community, of course, but in Argentina this loyalty is carried to such an extreme that the family is considered practically the *only* institution on which an individual can depend, and at the same time the only institution towards which an Argentine feels obligation and (almost always) manifests loyalty.

This is to some extent a "chicken-and-egg" problem. It is very difficult to know whether loyalty to the family is the cause or a result of a basic distrust in people outside the family's (and close friends') inner circle. At any rate, one characteristic is clear: the Argentine is what Ortega y Gasset calls "a man upon the defensive." He is acutely aware that any advantage that may be given to somebody outside his family is necessarily at the expense of himself and his own family. He will value gains accruing to the community only insofar as he and his are likely to share them. Similarly, he will feel a deep imperative to preserve what he has already gained or achieved for himself and his family. This automatically leads to nepotism in business and industry, family-run enterprises, reluctance to delegate authority and responsibilities, and unwillingness to dispense or share wealth with institutions other than one's own family.

The Argentine "Conglomeration"

The immoderate appetite for fortune, boldness, incompetence, and lack of adherence to and love for any trade or job are recognized characteristics endemic in any trading post. And it is precisely this set of characteristics which distinguishes the abstract and alluvial society of a trading post from a native, organic society.[27]

In conformance with our theoretical assumptions, what we call the

[27] *Ibid.*, p. 671; as quoted in Hanke, L.: *op. cit.*, p. 151.

Argentine "national character" has been defined by describing the value-orientation profile of the Argentine society. Two characteristics emerge clearly: first, that the dominant value orientations of the Argentine population are basically *passive;* second, that this particular value-orientation profile is inimical to the emergence of social relationships which would enable individuals to act concertedly in the pursuit of common goals. This characteristic, in turn, constitutes a powerful barrier to the appearance of economic initiative (in the Western-capitalistic sense) and of some degree of co-operation and unselfishness in the development of economic, social, and political enterprises. The immediate effect of these cultural characteristics upon the structure of the Argentine society can be best depicted by quoting H. A. Murena's commentaries on the nature of the "Argentine crisis."

> *There is no community in Argentina.* We do not form a body, though we may form a *conglomeration.* We behave as if each one were unique and as if he were alone, with the unfortunate consequences which result when that is the situation. The hand knoweth not what the head thinketh, the mouth ignoreth the stomach, "et cetera". . . . When a situation cannot be resolved within the framework of the community, then there must be a revolution, in order to modify that framework. Party struggles and revolution are the resources which assure the community of life. Instead of life, Argentina has rancorous, factious chaos, periodically illuminated by "coups d'état." It is not an organism of which all feel themselves a part. *Each organ believes itself the whole, and functions as if it were more important than the whole.* Is there any more succinct definition of sickness? Who is to blame? No one. Everyone.[28]

Murena also suggests that what he calls the "Argentine crisis" may have developed over the last hundred years or so. In his own words, there was during the nineteenth century at least an "animal instinct" which carried the country onward in spite of itself. During the last few decades, however, even this instinct seems to have disappeared. The only force which could have taken its place, a *community spirit,* was never formed. Murena's suggestion seems to us fundamentally accurate. The sequence of historical events since the foundation of the Argentine society suggests that its value-orientation profile may have deteriorated (from the point of view of community relationships and economic development) from being moderately passive to being unconcerned and apathetic over the last 150 years or so.[29] In the following section we will

[28] In "Notas sobre la Crisis Argentina," *Sur.,* No. 248 (Buenos Aires, 1957), pp. 1–16; partially reprinted in Hanke, L.: *op. cit.,* pp. 159–161. (Italics supplied.)

[29] The author briefly discusses this topic in *Industrial Relations in the Economic Development of Argentina,* S.M. thesis, unpublished (Massachusetts Institute of Technology, 1960), pp. 204–210. It should be noted here, however, that the gradual deterioration of

explore whether there are forces in *today's* society which would conceivably tend to produce a change in its dominant value orientations in the foreseeable future.

CONTINUITY THROUGH TIME

There has been no description in preceding pages of the *need structure* of the Argentine. The reason is simple and has already been stated in the first part of this chapter: there is nothing in the nature of personality which causes a *necessary* association between certain needs and certain value orientations. Hence, there is theoretically no reason to believe that the bulk of individuals within a society will tend to have a similar need structure.

On the other hand, there is evidence — both theoretical and empirical — that at least *some* needs may be fairly widespread and culturally transmitted in any given society.[30] In the case of the Argentine society, we think that this is true of at least two such needs: *"need aggression"* and *"need dependency."*

In simple terms, "need aggression" can be defined as a characteristic of the individual's personality which makes such an individual feel satisfaction from the act of being aggressive in thought or action, from attacking others and overcoming real or imaginary opposition forcefully. "Need dependency" is that characteristic of an individual's personality which makes one feel satisfaction from having ideas and attitudes approved by another person or persons, from having someone else to depend on rather than analyzing a problem and making rational choices oneself. (It should be noted that in accordance with common psychological terminology, we will here omit the preposition *for* — need *for* aggression, need *for* dependency — in referring to needs.)

The *"need aggression"* of the Argentine is perhaps his most obvious personality trait. It shows itself in a child's play, in soccer matches, on the streets, in one's driving habits, in politics, at work, and at home. Two examples are cited here:

> A stranger, first seeing a pair of Argentines in conversation, often feels that an explosion is imminent. To Argentines, a good rousing argument is a

---

the Argentine basic personality since the second half of the nineteenth century may have been due to the natives' defensive (and unconscious) drive to assert their individual worth and that of their culture, as the latter was looked down upon, or attacked, by culturally more actively oriented immigrants and, especially, American and Western European businessmen.

[30] See, for instance, E. E. Hagen: *op. cit.,* Chapter IV ff. The discussion that follows is based on theories expounded in Professor Hagen's manuscript.

vital .part of living. They like talk for talk's sake. Contradicting one's
friends or enemies is routine. . . .

Relatively few Argentines have any sense of public politeness. They frequently bump into people while scurrying round town, refusing all written
or unwritten rules about keeping to the right or left, or giving the right
of way to man, beast, or vehicle. . . .[31]

It should be stressed, however, that such behavior, being determined
partly by the Argentine's "need aggression" and partly by his compelling
drive to prove to himself that he *Is* something or somebody, by no means
contradicts our assertion that his "basic personality" is *passive*. Much has
been said and written about the "innate" *apathy* of the Argentine. This
apathy is actually a means of suppressing his "need aggression," a cover
for the anxiety and intense rage which must arise in a society built on
authoritarian values. Parallel to apathy, as a further effect of the
individual's feeling of *impotence* to attain his goals, sadness and
melancholy are also likely to appear. Indeed, we have seen that these
are common external traits of the Argentine, despite the fact that his
overt behavior is very often "aggressive." By means of such behavior,
the individual is partially discharging his rage and anxiety in a manner
which is, to a certain extent, sanctioned by his society. His value orientations, however, remain *passive*.

The Argentine's high *"need dependency"* can be best described with
one word: Perón. There is, however, a more fundamental reason to
believe in our assertion. According to Professor Hagen, an individual with
high "need dependency" will seek to be either in a position where someone is giving him complete guidance, or in one where he is in complete and
unquestioned authority. Namely, a strong "need dependency" can be satisfied in two different ways. One way is by finding a person who will make
all decisions — in political life a *Führer* or strong man — so that the individual who follows will not have to face problems without guidance or
need not make important, rational choices or decisions himself. For individuals who simultaneously show high "need aggression," the fit is
complete if the leader singles out an outside enemy who is accused, with
or without grounds, of threatening and belittling the follower or group
of followers, and against whom such followers may safely satisfy their
aggressive drives. The other method by which an individual may satisfy
his "need dependency" (and simultaneously his "need aggression")
is by being in absolute and undisputed command of those around him.
In such case, the anxiety of having to make rational choices and solving
problems by himself is relieved by the fact that there is no uncertainty
in the individual's environment, there are actually no problems to be

[31] Bruce, J.: *op. cit.*, pp. 28 and 30.

faced — one's choices and wishes, however irrational, are realized simply by ordering them to be fulfilled by persons around oneself. The preceding description perfectly fits the Argentine, his political behavior over the last 150 years, and his behavior in a situation of authority at work — be it in industry, in rural activities, or in public administrative offices. An individual with high "need dependency" has learned to handle interpersonal relations only in terms of power. A situation he has never learned to handle is one in which he faces someone else with the power situation unsettled and must negotiate a relationship by learning to understand the other person. Such a situation cannot be admissible and therefore frightens him. This is exactly what Ortega y Gasset means when he calls the Argentine a "man upon the defensive":

> In a normal interpersonal situation the Argentine does not abandon himself; on the contrary, when a fellow man approaches him, he seals in his soul and puts himself upon the defensive. . . . But we ask ourselves, against what, or against whom does he defend himself, if we do not attack him? This is precisely the peculiarity which most surprises his interlocutor. It is perfectly comprehensible that one should defend oneself when attacked; but to live in a state of siege when nobody harasses us is indeed a superlatively strange tendency.[32]

The above exposition makes it fairly obvious that an individual with high "need aggression" and high "need dependency" will tend to be an extremely autocratic superior and, at the same time, an overtly dutiful and obedient subordinate. But he will also tend to be an autocratic father and an obedient son. As a father, he will tend to discharge his anxiety and his aggressive needs on his children. Of course, he does it in complete innocence that he is thereby venting his rage. He is (culturally) convinced that every family must have a head who is obeyed. Indeed, a father who has no authority over his family or a husband who has none over his wife is laughed at or despised in Argentina. Furthermore, by completely controlling his children he is obviously protecting them. Thus he has a perfect rationalization for his attitude of absolute command over his family. At the same time, however, and again unwittingly, he is apt to be arbitrary, inconsistent, and unpredictable in the treatment of his children. Such attitudes may inculcate in the child a feeling that he is not valued, that it is reasonable to handle interpersonal situations in terms of power, and above all, that the world around him is unmanageable, that its responses to his actions are random, and thus that he is not responsible for such reactions or, indeed, for his behavior.

Of course, the mechanism of personality formation is certainly not *that*

[32] Ortega y Gasset, J.: *op. cit.,* p. 668.

simple. There are whole arrays of factors which have been left out of the picture and which may, in certain cases, partially mitigate or indeed reinforce the process of personality formation as described above. For our purposes, however, it is an accurate enough outline of one of the major mechanisms through which the depicted father's needs and value orientations may be transmitted *unmodified* to his son. Another such mechanism, the *identification* of a child with his father, will not be discussed at length here. It will suffice to point out that this process is not merely one of imitating the father. The child actually incorporates into his own personality values, attitudes, and standards of conduct which are part of the image of his father that he has created.

This identification process will be more complete the more the acquired values and beliefs fit one's experiences and perception of the outer world. In a situation like the Argentine, the probability that later events will *reinforce* earlier acquired beliefs and orientations is indeed great. From a man's first job on, for instance, be it in an *estancia* (the Argentine cattle ranch), in manufacturing, or in the service industries, he will perceive that his superiors are, as expected, autocratic, arbitrary (at least so he thinks, since nothing is explained to him), inconsistent, and unpredictable. Furthermore, since no responsibilities are given to him, his feeling of not being valued will be reinforced, and so will his beliefs that the world around him is unmanageable, that it responds at random to his actions.

With respect to an Argentine's community life, his childhood experiences have inculcated in him the feeling that suspicion is the reasonable attitude towards the world. In his contacts with it, he will indeed encounter diffident people, owing to the fact that the attitude of mistrust towards one's neighbor is a cultural characteristic. Such people, furthermore, will be the more distrustful the more patent his initial attitude of suspicion.

These are two examples which could be extended *ad infinitum*. The important fact to realize is that, conceptually, *such a society is basically static with respect to changes in the value orientations of its members;* this, we believe, is the case in contemporary Argentine society.[33]

IMMIGRATION

We cannot conclude this chapter on the Argentine national character without some reference to the impact of immigration waves on the

[33] In accordance with our simple model, a change in the value-orientation profile of the society can only be conceived as a development towards higher degrees of passivity. Indeed, such a process seems to have taken place in the past. To take into consideration this possibility, however, would only complicate our exposition while by no means modifying our approach to Argentina's economic development.

Argentine society. This topic merits special consideration because, contrary to the opinions of many authors, we believe that immigration has not had a *radical* influence on the cultural characteristics of the Argentine society, although it has drastically changed the ethnic composition of the population. This ethnic change, moreover, has led the majority of Argentines to believe that their society lacks stability as a result of the imperfect, or as yet incomplete, fusion of its two main elements: the energetic immigrant and the easygoing native. We maintain that the reasons for this instability, as well as for the failure of the Argentine society to take the road of steady and dynamic economic advance, must be looked for elsewhere — namely in the cultural characteristics of the *whole* population — because the degree of cultural assimilation of the bulk of the immigrant element into the native society has been great. More specifically, the degree of "goodness of fit" of the two elements' own basic value orientations has been too high to have made a two-way acculturation process at all necessary.

Immigration Waves and Social Mobility

During the second half of the nineteenth century, Argentina's economic progress, based on the exportation of meat, required the services of many more workers than had ever been needed to care for cattle in earlier periods. Thus, between 1857 and 1900, encouraged by liberal immigration policies, approximately 2,000,000 immigrants arrived in Buenos Aires. Although 800,000 departed during the same period — mainly Italians who traveled to Argentina for the Southern Hemisphere's harvest and then returned to Europe in time for the Italian wheat harvest — by 1905 the immigrant element amounted to 25.4 per cent of the country's total population. Almost 80 per cent of the newcomers were Italians and Spaniards (the former slightly outnumbering the latter). These immigrants brought agriculture to Argentina. Large numbers of families settled in the plain regions and constituted the bulk of the farm population. It was this group, mainly northern Italians (southern Italians remained in the towns), but also Spanish and northern European immigrants, that made the *pampa* one of the world's leading surplus grain and meat regions. Unfortunately, however, and in spite of courage and hard labor, their dream of riches and prosperity did not usually come true. By the time they arrived, the pattern of land ownership was fixed. Spanish colonists during the seventeenth and eighteenth centuries and native governments later on had already divided the land into huge, privately owned *estancias*. For the immigrant, *tenancy* was practically the only way of life, since land in small units for sale at reasonable prices was practically unavailable. Tenants did not live on a relatively low level physically: food, clothing, and shelter were fairly adequate. The cultural components of living, however, were on a low level for the tenants. They lacked educational opportunities, community life, and social and recreational activities.[34]

The fortunes of those immigrants who settled in urban centers did not follow the same pattern. They provided the necessary manpower to permit the emergence of a large "middle sector," constituting today at least 45 per cent of the Argentine population. [35] Until approximately 1880, the middle sector formed only a small minority, and its composition was essentially static: professionals, professors, bureaucrats, members of the clergy and of the officer corps. As long as the demands for these skills rose gradually, as was the case during the 1880's, the increment to middle-sector positions came almost wholly from their own ranks. By the turn of the century, however, the start of industrial activities, together with the expansion of education, commerce, and of the functions of the state, opened the doors of social advancement to lower groups, especially to the immigrant elements among them. By the early 1900's *80 per cent* of the owners of commercial and industrial establishments were immigrants or naturalized citizens, a high percentage of which were obviously of working class background.

After the 1890 economic crisis, which resulted in a net loss of population, immigration resumed on an even larger scale, although it showed cyclical characteristics. Peaks were reached in 1896, 1913, and — after a prolonged interruption caused primarily by World War I — 1929. The number of immigrants who arrived in Buenos Aires and remained in the country between 1900 and 1930 totaled 2,900,000, again nearly 80 per cent of them being of either Italian or Spanish nationality. By 1914, 29.3 per cent of the total population were native Europeans. By 1935, this figure had dwindled to 20.4 per cent. Between 1930 and 1947, because of severe governmental restrictions, immigration was brought virtually to a standstill. But between 1947 and 1953, Perón's immigration policies resulted in a net inflow of 522,000 immigrants, nearly 62 per cent of them Italians. Thereafter, new restrictions were imposed on immigration. It is also interesting to note that, since the turn of the century, more and more immigrants have

[34] Ortiz, R.: *Historia Económica de la Argentina* (Buenos Aires, Editorial Raigal, 1955, 2 Vols.); Hanson, S.: *Economic Development in Latin America* (Washington, The Inter-American Affairs Press, 1951), esp. pp. 85–86; and Taylor, C.: *Rural Life in Argentina* (Louisiana State University Press, 1948).

[35] The expression "middle sector" will be used in this book to identify what is usually referred to as a "middle class" because of the total absence of cohesion or "class-consciousness" among the members of the Argentine middle strata. Publications of international agencies commonly fix this sector as constituting 50 per cent of the nation's total population. Main sources for our discussion of the middle sectors have been Germani, G.: "Algunas Repercusiones Sociales de los Cambios Económicos en la Argentina," summarized in *Ciencias Sociales* (Pan American Union, Vol. III, no. 18, Dec. 1952), pp. 147–158; and Johnson, J. J.: *Political Change in Latin America* (Stanford, California, Stanford University Press, 1958).

remained in and around Argentina's urban centers. During the period 1947–1953 practically all immigrants settled in Greater Buenos Aires.[36]

Through the initial decades of this century, the growth of the middle sectors was even greater than it had been at the turn of the century. While by 1895 it constituted an estimated 32 per cent of the total economically active population, it reached 43 per cent in 1936. The main source of vertical mobility, however, differed from that of the previous period. Specifically, during the period between world wars, it became much less common for people to enter the middle sectors by becoming owners of commercial or industrial establishments, while the professions and the bureaucracy (private and public) stood out as the main source of vertical rise. This situation directly affected immigrant entrepreneurship: by 1935, 45 per cent of all industrial owners were Argentine-born, the percentage increasing to 60 by 1947. Actually, during and after World War II, the process of vertical mobility diminished greatly. In its place, horizontal — occupational and geographical — mobility within the lower social groups took the lead as a source of social transformation. This was primarily due to the expansion of industrial activities during that period. The number of workers employed in industrial establishments rose by 87 per cent between 1938 and 1947. By the latter year, the middle sectors represented slightly more than 43 per cent and the workers nearly 54 per cent of the total economically active population — practically no change with respect to 1936. Furthermore, industrialization had greatly contributed to a drastic change in the occupational distribution of the population: the proportion of rural population to total population had dwindled from 63 per cent in 1895 to 39 per cent in 1947.

These trends were greatly accentuated by Perón's income redistribution policies. In fact, the transformation of the Argentine economic structure after 1943 had different repercussions among the various occupational sectors of the population. Proprietors of industry and commerce obtained the proportionately greatest share of benefits; at least until 1948, real industrial wages also showed a steady upward trend; on the other hand, the agricultural, professional, and real-estate groups as well as the bureaucracy saw their real incomes shrink alarmingly. The consequent leveling of economic differences between the lower and the middle sectors obviously removed many incentives for social advancement. Under such circumstances, a decrease in the society's vertical mobility is perfectly understandable.

One particular characteristic of the development of the middle lay-

---

[36] Sources are Ortiz, R.: *op. cit.,* Vols. I and II; Pendle, G.: *op. cit.;* and James, P. E.: *Latin America* (New York, The Odyssey Press, 1959), Chapter 9.

ers should be stressed: in Argentina the middle sector is large, but it does not provide the stabilizing influence which a middle class is usually expected to provide wherever it develops. The reason is that the Argentine middle sectors are in themselves anything but a compact social layer. In fact, they do not constitute a united, coherent class, but rather "an aggregation of disparate groups and individuals who have little in common beyond the fact that they occupy a middle position between the oligarchy above and the [working class] beneath." [37] Their members have no common background, since Spanish, Italian, and other European immigrant elements and their descendants share this social position with the original nucleus of old Spanish and creole families. Rapidly growing white-collar groups of shopkeepers, clerks, and bureaucrats coexist with professionals, industrialists, and property owners. Some are members of the middle sector because of their education and intellectual attainments; others, more because of their wealth than because of their learning. Some have only recently risen from lower levels of society; others have inherited a traditional contempt for labor and the labor movement; still others have only a paternalistic interest in the working elements. Politically, the middle sectors do not constitute the major force that they undoubtedly would if they shared a common social background and similar economic interests. From our point of view, however, they are of prime interest because it is from their ranks that all levels of the managerial and administrative force are, and will continue to be, drawn.

It has often been said that, historically, Argentina has been a highly mobile society. Undoubtedly, as our discussion in preceding pages suggests, this assertion is true with respect to social mobility between the middle and lower layers. There is also enough evidence that, *economically,* Argentina has been a fairly open society, since it has given the opportunity of economic advancement to all its members (for brevity's sake, we choose to overlook the obvious barriers to personal economic advancement which have existed in the agricultural and stock-raising sectors of the economy). But from the point of view of the attainment of social and — up to the early forties — political power, Argentina can certainly not be described as an open society. It would be fundamentally wrong to assume that because they have held since the mid-forties the control of the economic and political life of the nation, the new commercial, financial, and industrial élites are part of Argentina's "upper class," together with the old landowning aristocracy. Certainly, the situation is slowly — and fortunately

[37] Whitaker, A.: *The United States and Argentina* (Cambridge, Mass., Harvard University Press, 1954), p. 13. See also pp. 204–208 for a more detailed account of the impact of Perón's policies on the distribution of income.

— changing; but, at least as Argentines themselves see it, the "upper class" is still the nation's old patrician class. Its core has always been made up of the large landowners, particularly of those engaged in stock raising, the *estancieros*.

Throughout the Perón era (1946–1955) and in spite of the landowners' abrupt loss of control over the political life of the nation, the aristocracy maintained its social structure basically intact. Economically, Perón's policies hurt large landowners the most. By the end of the dictatorship, the economic disparity between the wealthy few and the needy masses had not disappeared; but wealth had changed hands. Of course, part of it had left the country in the hands of the fugitive *peronista* hierarchy. But a new, wealthy commercial and industrial élite, the chief beneficiary of Argentina's economic transformation, had also emerged — more accurately, had seen consolidated the economic power it had been building up since the 1930's. In spite of these changes, most of the aristocracy still looks down — consciously or unconsciously — upon industry and business, for the cultural reasons which have already been explored. One is forced to believe that as long as this attitude persists, the role which the landed élite may play in modern Argentina's expanding economy is likely to diminish.

Against this background, let us now explore the role which immigration may have played in influencing the Argentine society's value-orientation profile.

Immigrant Acculturation

Every process of immigrant acculturation involves two closely related phenomena: on the one hand, the assimilation of the immigrant group into the native society; on the other, the reaction of the native society to the (welcome or unwelcome) intrusion of an alien group into it. The relative importance of one such phenomenon with respect to the other depends mainly (although not exclusively) on the number, economic influence, political power, and social prestige of the immigrant group, relative to the native society. Furthermore, it is obvious that, first, regardless of their relative importance, *both* aspects of the process are necessarily found in every case of immigrant acculturation; second, both phenomena take place simultaneously, and they are closely related to, and exert powerful influence on, each other. Therefore, it is only for purposes of a more convenient analysis that we will consider in the following discussion each of the two aspects of immigrant acculturation separately. We must, however, keep in mind that the features of each phenomenon simultaneously influence, and are influenced by, those of the other.

Of all immigrants to Argentina, we will here consider Italians and

Spaniards as the only numerically strong group of newcomers which, lacking at the time of their arrival any economic or political power, might have conceivably played some role in modifying, by the sheer weight of their number, the value-orientation profile of the native society. It is empirically evident that non-Latin immigrants, enjoying absolute personal liberty, have often succeeded in forming tight colonies where even today they preserve their language, the customs of their ancestors, and their religion. Owing to this largely self-imposed isolation and to the fact that such groups have historically constituted only small minorities among immigration waves, we will here assume that, except in those few cases where individual members represented or acquired economic power, non-Latin immigrant groups have played in the past a negligible role as agents of social change. Of course, the same cannot be said of Italian and Spanish immigrants, who by themselves constitute roughly 80 per cent of total immigration figures.

Let us now turn to a separate analysis of the two aspects of the process of immigrant acculturation, as it applies to the Argentine society.[38]

The main element to be considered in discussing the process of assimilation of immigrant groups into the Argentine society is the degree to which their value orientations differ from those of the bulk of the Argentine population.[39] In the case of Spanish and Italian immigrants, we suggest that such differences were not great. At least up until 1930, the bulk of Spanish and Italian immigrants were low-income members of peasant cultures. We cannot analyze here the ethos of such societies. But we can draw some general conclusions out of the studies of eminent investigators, based on Redfield's suggestion that, at least with respect to Mediterranean societies, common central characteristics of culture are found in all past and present peasant societies.[40] Hagen [41] points out that the personality of the bulk of the members of most peasant societies in equilibrium (or "quasi-equilibrium") is typically characterized by an insatiable "need dependency," low "need autonomy" (need to be independent of control by others), low "need achievement" (satisfaction from solving problems),

[38] The discussion that follows is largely based on concepts and ideas presented in Hagen, E. E.: *op. cit.*, Ch. VII–X.

[39] We are here generalizing and applying to the Argentine society Dr. F. Kluckhohn's hypothesis that "the rate and degree of assimilation of any ethnic group into general dominant American culture will in large part depend upon the degree of goodness of fit of the group's own basic value orientations with those of dominant American culture" (*op. cit.*, p. 354). It seems evident that the main reason for the at best incomplete acculturation of non-Latin immigrant elements is the incompatibility of their value orientations with those dominant in the Argentine society. It is, however, beyond the scope of this monograph to elaborate further on this point.

[40] Redfield, R.: *Peasant Society and Culture* (Chicago, University of Chicago Press, 1956).

[41] Hagen, E. E.: *op. cit.*, esp. Ch. VII.

a rather constricting degree of "need order" (need to be neat, orderly), and pervasive rage coupled with an intense "need aggression." More importantly, however, the personality of such an individual will be further characterized by an *extremely passive "world view"* (a term defining how an individual regards the physical world and one's social position in it, and which encompasses his value orientations, his preferences, and his cognitive image of the world). Finally, peasant societies will usually be organized on the basis of a rigid social structure, with all power in the hands of a largely hereditary élite.

The striking similarity between such a typical peasant society and some aspects of the Argentine society is, of course, no accident. The men who originally settled Argentina were not rebels against the existing social order in Europe, as was the case in the United States. They sailed to Argentine shores to search for treasures. They were so sure they would find them that they gave the name of Río de la Plata (River of Silver or River Plate) to a brown, ugly estuary. They came to exploit the country and to extend the control of the Spanish Crown and the Church into the newly discovered lands. Thus, the Argentine society was founded on the same social organizational patterns prevailing in Spain — on the assumption that a society consists of a natural hierarchical order in which a few are born to rule and many are born to serve. Thus, together with a social structure built upon dominance and subordination, Argentines "inherited" all Spanish cultural characteristics — among others, their passive "world view." After the achievement of political independence Argentina developed into an economically — if not socially and politically — highly mobile society. But its *dominant* cultural characteristics remained basically unchanged, as witnessed by Argentina's history as an independent republic. *Prima facie,* the cultural differences between native Argentines and post-1850 immigrants must have therefore been too small to permit the initiation of a two-way acculturation process which would have exerted lasting influence on the value-orientation profile of the Argentine society. In other words, the cultural assimilation of the bulk of the immigrant element has been complete because of the high degree of goodness of fit of the basic value orientations of the two groups (immigrants and native society).

We must, however, take into account the fact that a considerable number of immigrants during the period 1857–1930 must have been deviant members of their original society, in one sense or another social rebels. Leaving aside the fact that within a traditional peasant society, the degree of social deviance of individual members is usually bound to be small,[42] it is conceivable that such individuals, possessing more active value orientations than the average immigrant, might not have been completely assimi-

[42] *Ibid.,* Ch. IX.

lated into the Argentine society. Thus they would establish within the society a numerically large focus of deviance, which, under favorable circumstances, could have spurred the nation's social change and the rate and vigor of its economic growth. We shall now try to explain why this has largely not been the case.

A social rebel surely resents (consciously or unconsciously) the fact that his society will not accept him on his terms. But the immigrant is also sufficiently motivated to solve his problem, and thus he strikes out by emigrating rather than retreating into apathy as other members of his society do. Therefore, it is logical to believe that besides his drive for autonomy and achievement, some degree of "need aggression" must be conspicuous in him. To the extent that he is successful in satisfying his drive for achievement in the new society, he will be apt to feel free to satisfy the other part of his ambivalent goal: the exercise of authority himself. This tendency must have greatly contributed to the founding of the autocratic system of management conspicuous in Argentine enterprises, the nation's industry being largely the product of immigrant entrepreneurship. Moreover, such an immigrant is also apt to be an autocratic father and pass his authoritarian personality on to his children in accordance with the mechanisms explained earlier in this chapter.

In addition, an immigrant who succeeds in attaining an economic position considerably above the one he held in his country of origin logically expects the new society to accord him the social status which people of comparable wealth and income held in his original society. In Argentina, however, the values attached to money and wealth are not those of other, less mobile societies. Money in itself is not a key to social recognition, as has been already pointed out. It is therefore logical to expect that the successful immigrant must have felt deprived of the social position he believed rightfully his own. Professor Hagen suggests that as a consequence of such or similar feelings, a progressive deterioration in the pursuit of goals over several generations may take place. Over the generations, if one's prowess cannot gain for one the recognition one feels he deserves, and if no route of escape from the trap seems open, a pervasive apathy associated with some degree of "retreatism" will become steadily more apparent, with ever-increasing amounts of anxiety attached to it. Furthermore, active value orientations will be progressively abandoned as a result of the individual's feeling of impotence to attain his (in our case, social) goals.

Through such a process, and in spite of being himself somewhat of a social rebel with respect to his original society, the successful immigrant to Argentina, or his descendants, acquired passive value orientations, which made his assimilation into the Argentine society complete. However, it is important to note that as long as the successful immigrant preserved all or part of his active value orientations, he was indeed able to contribute to the slow and stumbling advance of the Argentine economy; and that, therefore, each immigration wave brought new, short-lived, sources of limited economic growth.

Obviously, however, those newcomers who achieve their goals constitute only a minority of all immigrants. But even those immigrants who were unsuccessful in satisfying their drive for achievement must have been at least to some degree subject to a process similar to that depicted above. Practically all immigrants consciously or unconsciously seek in the new society the recognition they have been denied in their societies of origin. In Argentina, however, be it in urban or rural areas, they typically found a society which looked down upon them socially. And prominent within the disparaging group were those immigrants who had arrived during the previous or next-to-last immigration wave. The reasons for this phenomenon — which is, by the way, world-wide — will not be discussed here. But its consequences, which have been consistently pointed out by students of the Argentine society, are worth analyzing. It is characteristic of immigrants and especially their children to show a compulsive drive to demonstrate that they are more *Argentinos* than the Argentines themselves; thus they meticulously "ape" the native's overt behavior. By means of such a process, which is known in psychological theory as "identification with the aggressor," [43] the individual tries to persuade himself (usually unconsciously) that he is one with the disparaging groups and cannot therefore be in danger of losing his own identity. But this psychological maneuver requires the continued expenditure of energy and exposes the individual to continuous internal conflict. This, together with the frustration and disillusion he must feel for not having been able to realize his dreams of prosperity, riches, and social recognition, is apt to lead the individual (or his descendants) into eventual apathy or "retreatism" and cause him to assume progressively passive value orientations.

On the other hand, how did the native society react to the intrusion of alien groups into it? Did its value-orientation profile undergo a process of change, and if so, in what direction?

We will first analyze the reaction of the native society towards those energetic, economically successful immigrants who, as we have suggested, possessed at the time of their arrival more active value orientations than the average immigrant and the native society in general. From the point of view of our analysis, we must also include in this group those in-

---

[43] See Freud, Anna: *The Ego and the Mechanisms of Defence* (New York, International Universities Press, Inc., 11th Printing, 1960), pp. 118 ff.

dividuals who came to Argentine shores in connection with, and representing, foreign investments — mainly British, but also American, French, Belgian, German, and other foreign businessmen and technicians. These people entered the Argentine society invested with, or representing, great economic power, and monopolized for decades most key positions in large sectors of the Argentine economy (transportation, communication, utilities, trade, many manufacturing industries, banking, insurance, etc.). To the extent that they left their countries of origin only for a limited span of time, such "foreign capital representatives" were, technically speaking, not immigrants. Their economic power, however, may have given them an influence as (unwitting) agents of deterioration of native dominant value orientations greater than the influence of other numerically far more important immigrant groups.

It is obvious that the American and Western European businessmen who administered their own or their countrymen's investments in Argentina possessed generally very active value orientations. Typically, they demonstrated, if not outright contempt, at least marked condescension with regard to the native society, its values, and other cultural traits. This attitude, of course, is not a phenomenon which has been restricted to Argentina. It has existed in the past wherever Western powers achieved political or economic domination of the nonindustrialized, traditional societies of the world. Furthermore, it is clear that such an attitude usually has been assumed without conscious awareness, although such individuals probably must have been unconsciously compelled to belittle, or even despise as unworthy, the native culture and society to assuage their own feeling of guilt for denying the natives economic, social, and administrative status.[44] At any rate, since the sources of the contempt or condescension shown by these alien groups (and, to some extent, initially also by the group of economically successful immigrants) were their value orientations, the Argentine society reacted defensively by *rejecting* such alien (active) value orientations and by clinging the more compulsively to traditional (passive) ones. In effect, the preservation of the sense of identity of Argentine natives depended on the subsistence of those

---

[44] See Hagen, E. E.: *op. cit.,* Ch. IX. In Argentina, for instance, British capital "financed the railways, installed port facilities, gave Buenos Aires waterworks and street transportation, established department stores, improved banking and insurance and shipping machinery of commerce while participating directly in export and import trade. It became customary to call Argentina a British dependency economically. . . . [But] British capital tended to identify its interests with those of the great landowning and governing families, showed the same lack of concern with broadening of the internal market and with hastening of a general rise in the standard of living. . . . The tariff structure could be set up to protect the landowning group which was not enthusiastic about the growth of local industry. Local entrepreneurial ability . . . found very limited opportunities in the British ventures that kept key posts in British hands" (Hanson, S.: *op. cit.,* p. 381).

cultural characteristics which were looked down upon by the alien group. If they abandoned them, Argentines would have not had a valid basis for denying that the alien was of superior worth and that their own status as a people was subject to contempt. *Unconsciously,* they could therefore not accept the Western-capitalist attitude towards economic pursuits, the valuation of money as a source of social status, the prestige of industrial activities — more generally, a more active set of value orientations. On the contrary, in order to preserve their identity, it was imperative for them to emphasize and attach themselves the more strongly to traditional value orientations, attitudes, and preferences.

But Western culture, living standards, and social habits presented obvious advantages. Above all, Western societies held in their hands the world's economic and military power. *Consciously,* Argentines recognized the superiority of Western-capitalist culture and admitted that it was in their personal material interest (and, secondarily, in that of their country) to follow the kind of economic activities introduced by the alien. This, of course, constituted a practical way to gain enough strength to repel foreign intruders and regain dignity. They thus set out consciously to imitate Western habits and attitudes. Over several decades, such things as European clothing and mannerisms, the practice of British sports, Western educational standards and methods, a modern organization of trade and commerce, and eventually Western industrial activities took root in Argentine society.

The conscious imitation of values and attitudes, however, which the individual unconsciously abhors and seeks to reject is obviously a source of deep psychological conflict. The handling of such a conflict (akin to that arising from the previously mentioned mechanism of "identification with the aggressor") demands of the individual the perennial expenditure of energy and is a source of rage, anxiety, and apathy. Above all, it prevents the individual from taking part wholeheartedly and actively in those endeavors which he best identifies with the disparaging group and which most violate his traditional values and attitudes — in the Argentine case, industrial activities and all the social attitudes which go with them.

The consequences of the above-depicted social processes appear in every aspect of Argentine life. Two, however, are especially noteworthy.

First, always latent and ready to express themselves are the rage, rancor, and anxious feelings of the Argentine towards the economically powerful aliens and especially towards those among the latter who most grossly violate with their attitudes the value orientations of the Argentine people. Thus the anti-Americanism and especially the strong anti-British feelings of the Argentine population.

Secondly, Argentines have shown in recent years — probably since the late thirties — a conscious and apparently sincere desire for industrialization. As we have already mentioned, this desire is entirely consistent with the social mechanisms we have previously described. But so are the results. Argentines have undertaken the imitation of Western industrial activities without drive or conviction, stumblingly and uncreatively. A psychological commitment to, and rational pursuit of, the methods and objectives of industrialization programs are still largely absent; this is best demonstrated by the inclusion in Argentine industrialization programs of projects which are not economic (Perón's atomic-power adventures, for instance) and serve only to undermine the nation's energy and resources. These facts would indeed be taken into account by Argentine economic planners, and by the bulk of the population, were it not for their compelling unconscious drive for power and dominance without embracing the values and attitudes — or going through the preparatory stages of social transformation — of a modern industrial society.

So much with respect to the reaction of the Argentine society towards foreign businessmen and the economically successful immigrant. But what about its reaction to the intrusion of the mass of Spanish and Italian immigrants?

To the extent that the latter possessed value orientations as passive as those of the Argentines, which we have previously suggested has been largely the case, a defensive maneuver of the above-depicted type has been unnecessary. Numerically, however, immigrants presented somewhat of a threat. They were prepared to accept any kind of job and were generally more energetic than the natives. They spoke a different language (or Spanish in a different way) and had somewhat different habits and ideals. Furthermore, they were the same kind of people as the other economically successful immigrants, who looked askance at native values and attitudes. But, at the same time, the mass of immigrants obviously lacked social prestige and political or economic power. And the natives were certainly not ready and willing to surrender to, or share with, the newcomers such power and prestige. Since they had no great achievements to justify this attitude, and in order to preserve their sense of worth as individuals and as a nation, the natives necessarily had to assume (unconsciously) that they were a superior, more worthy people than the immigrants. Thus, they looked down upon the newcomer, his habits, energy, attitudes, and where present his somewhat more active value orientations.

Before drawing some general conclusions from this analysis of immigrant acculturation in Argentina, we must again stress that the two separate processes according to which we have divided our discussion occur simultaneously and are closely dependent upon each other. Furthermore, it is obvious that we have focused our analysis on the general aspects of such processes; we are, however, perfectly aware that our analysis and conclusions may not apply to particular cases and individuals.

In general, we can conclude that the Argentine society has assimilated the impact of massive immigration without undergoing a noticeable change in its value-orientation profile. If such a change has occurred at all, it has been mainly caused by the influx of foreign capital; and it has resulted probably in a deterioration (from an economic-development standpoint), at least in a stiffening, of its passive value-orientation profile. Meanwhile, as we shall see in the following chapter, the Argentine economy grew and progressed, mainly because of the strength of its traditional farming and export sectors, the initial impetus of each new wave of immigrants, and most importantly the technical and administrative contribution of foreign capital. But this development process occurred slowly, unsteadily, and with difficulty. In addition to many other factors, its strength has greatly diminished with the fading away of immigrant impetus (following the mechanisms of assimilation previously described) and with the unavailability of foreign capital in response to Argentine or international events.

Before undertaking a brief analysis of those other factors which have prevented the Argentine economy from taking the road of steady economic growth, we should pose a question which bears on the future of Argentine economic development. The question is the following: Now that immigrant entrepreneurs have been assimilated into the society, now that they (or their descendants) have adopted the general pattern of value orientations and are therefore considered by the traditional member of the society to be "one of mine," now that their road to economic success can be imitated without the danger of losing one's own worth and one's sense of identity, may not some Argentines *wholeheartedly* choose industry as the surest and most plausible way to get ahead in their society? Although we lack any empirical evidence, we are inclined to believe that such a process may be presently taking place in Argentina.

3 THE ARGENTINE ECONOMY

In this chapter we shall consider the main causes of Argentina's economic stagnation, and thus the main barriers to the nation's economic growth. It is our contention that these are of a social character rather than purely economic as has been widely assumed. Of course, this does not mean that there are and have been no economic (or, for that matter, political) problems to solve in Argentina; or that such problems are and have been few or rather unimportant. It would be unrealistic to state that one element alone is the cause of the nation's current period of economic stagnation. Actually, all imaginable impediments are reciprocally related: each is both a cause and a consequence of all others. The main purpose of this chapter is to show that *the cultural characteristics of the Argentine society* have been in the past, and will continue to be in the future, the *critical* factor governing the nature, and limiting the degree and continuity, of the nation's economic development.

Social Background

For all practical purposes, the development of modern Argentina's economy may be said to have started in 1853 with the fall of Juan Manuel de Rosas' dictatorship (1829–1852) and the enactment of the 1853 Constitution. There are, however, some features inherited from the period before 1853 which must not be overlooked if the profound changes that followed are to be understood.

During the years of colonization, Spanish settlers divided the land into huge tracts where herds of horses, sheep, and cattle were pastured with a minimum of attention from the owners. The necessary work was performed mainly by hired natives of pure Spanish or half-Indian origin. But neither the landowners nor the *gauchos* were agricultural people. When wheat farming was introduced by immigrants and the pampas proved to be land of first-rate quality for such activities, agriculture was encouraged by the landlords as a by-product of the expansion and improvement of grazing activities. But grain farming itself as well as the tenants (mostly immigrants) who carried on such activity were still looked down upon by the vast majority of original settlers.

Nobody has better described Argentina's social situation during the first decades of its existence as an independent nation than Domingo F. Sarmiento in his classic *Facundo*,[1] first published in 1845. For Sarmiento, young Argentina represented a violent struggle between *civilización* and *barbarie*. He recognized in his society, as a perpetual threat to the stability of the nation, the simultaneous and contradictory presence of, on the one hand, all the elements of "civilization" — moral values, learning, wealth — on the other, all the elements of "barbarism" — brutality, ignorance, poverty. Above all, he realized that the forces of barbarism could as readily take control of the Argentine society as could those of civilization. Indeed, throughout the first half of the nineteenth century, the country alternated between decency and degradation, the "barbarous" remaining the major force in the fledgling Argentine society. The uncivilized masses found their spokesmen and leaders in a host of anarchic Provincial *caudillos,* most of them ruthless butchers, and in the greatest *caudillo* of them all, the tyrant Rosas, who ruled the country for more than twenty years. Those were not only years of moral degradation; they represented a clear step backwards in the cultural, political, and economic development of the nation, a period of total stagnation which would only repeat itself a hundred years later, under very similar circumstances.

According to José Manuel Estrada, the struggle between civilization and barbarism (or "the intellectuals" and "the masses," in Estrada's terms) lasted beyond the fall of Rosas in 1852 and the enactment of the 1853 Constitution, when some form of stable unity was eventually achieved throughout the Argentine territory.[2] But once the immediate danger of anarchy had disappeared, *i.e.,* once Argentina's existence as a united nation was reasonably assured, the ruling classes (among which it is hardly possible to differentiate "intellectuals" and the landowning aristocracy) attempted, successfully, to exclude the masses from participation in the affairs of the state. The reasons for this attitude are clear: they are to be found in what we have described as the "basic personality" of the Argentine — reluctance to delegate authority, emphasis on Being, prestige of the landowners, etc. Thus, Argentina evolved

[1] *Facundo, Civilización y Barbarie* (Universidad Nacional de La Plata, Alberto Pacos, ed., 1938).
[2] Estrada, J. M.: *La Política Liberal bajo la Tiranía de Rosas* (published as Vol. LXXXIII in the series Grandes Escritores Argentinos, Alberto Palcos, ed., Buenos Aires, 1925). See also Kennedy, J.: *Catholicism, Nationalism and Democracy in Argentina* (Notre Dame, Ind., University of Notre Dame Press, 1958), pp. 30–35.

slowly at first, but rapidly after 1880 (when the city of Buenos Aires was ultimately brought under the jurisdiction of the national government), in the direction of "civilization," that is, following the road marked by the aristocracy and the intellectuals, the sole holders of all political power in the nation. This made it possible for Argentina to conserve internal peace while growing from a small, sparsely populated country into an important modern nation *developed according to the values and needs of the ruling élite.* Beneath the apparent apathy — political and otherwise — of the masses, however, rage, anxiety, and aggression steadily mounted. This is shown in their rebellious outbursts each time they have had a reasonable chance of success. Needless to say that Perón, the only leader who seems to have really known how to turn their raw power into the dominant force in society, provided them with such a chance. So did Irigoyen, who was twice elected to the Presidency in 1916 and 1928. It is however important to realize that the difference in the degree of participation the masses were allowed or were able to take in the affairs of the nation under each of the two leaders established the difference between moderate economic progress and total economic collapse. But let us first explore what we mean by an economy developed according to the values and needs of the ruling élite.

EARLY PERIODS

The development of the Argentine grasslands grew *pari passu* with the construction of the means of transportation, mainly railroads. The first Argentine railroad, the Ferrocarril del Oeste, started operations in 1857. It was financed by public and private Argentine capital, constructed and operated by Argentines.[3] The example of this group of pioneers, however, was not to be followed by the wealthy *estancieros,* who were either unable or unwilling to invest their capital in railway

---

[3] Scalabrini Ortiz, R.: *Historia de los Ferrocarriles Argentinos* (Buenos Aires, Ed. Devenir, 1957), p. 27.

The analysis of the Argentine economy presented in this section is based on the following sources:

Defelippe, B.: *Geografía Económica Argentina.* Buenos Aires, Ed. Losange, 1959.
DiTella, G.: *Economic History of Argentina; 1914–1933.* Ph.D. thesis, Massachusetts Institute of Technology, 1960, unpublished.
Ortiz, R.: *Historia Económica de la Argentina,* 2 Vols. Buenos Aires, Ed. Raigal, 1955.
United Nations, C.E.P.A.L.: *El Desarrollo Económico de la Argentina,* Part I (Mexico, 1959).
United Nations, *Economic Bulletin for Latin America,* Vol. IV, No. 1 (Santiago, Chile, March 1959), pp. 13–24.
Zymelman, M.: *The Economic History of Argentina (1933–1952).* Ph.D. thesis, Massachusetts Institute of Technology, 1958, unpublished.

ventures. At the same time, foreign (mainly British) investors saw an opportunity for huge profits in a rapidly expanding economy. Thus, Great Britain supplied most of the capital, technicians, coal, and equipment necessary for the development of railroads. By 1890, the Argentine government even sold to a British concern the only large Argentine-owned railroad — the Ferrocarril del Oeste. For all practical purposes, the Argentine railway system was in foreign hands. And its further development was naturally geared to the necessities of foreign rather than local markets, of stock raising and agriculture rather than industry.

The railroad and the invention of the refrigerator ship not only transformed the pampa (and "virtually harnessed [it] to the economy of far-away Great Britain"[4]) but also brought unheard-of prosperity to Argentine landowners, in whose hands wealth remained highly concentrated. Furthermore, on the basis of an oligarchical and corrupt political system, the aristocracy also maintained firm control of the government. Under such circumstances, no determined action was taken by the state to check the inflationary process which developed during the late 1880's: currency depreciation, of course, meant higher peso incomes received by the landowners for their exports. The crash occurred in 1890 and it stopped the first attempt at industrial development: meat packing, flour milling, beer brewing, the processing of tannin, and the making of carriages and matches were first undertaken during the 1880's. Industrial growth was only resumed with the opening of the port of Buenos Aires in 1901, and it took real impetus only during World War I because of the unavailability of foreign manufactures.

Two distinct features characterized this early industrialization process. First, it was nonspecialized, a pattern that Argentine industry has followed ever since. Second, and in perfect harmony with the growth process of the economy as a whole, industrial development was "externally directed"; in other words, the growth process was one of integration with the international market and adaptation of the production effort to world market supply and demand. In effect, because of the complementary character of the British and Argentine economies and the dominance of landed interests in the making of national policy, industry up to 1931 (when difficulties in export markets hastened adoption of a more vigorous protectionistic policy for local industry) was less actively supported by the government "than in countries where export interests were less actively concerned with promotion and maintenance of freer trade."[5] The government's tariff and exchange-

---

[4] Pendle, G.: *Argentina* (London, Oxford University Press, 1955), p. 46.
[5] Hanson, S.: *Economic Development in Latin America* (Washington, D.C., The Inter-American Affairs Press, 1951), p. 169.

control policies during those years has even been termed "protectionism in reverse" and "malevolent neutrality towards industry." Thus, many World War I industries were forced to shut down after the cessation of hostilities in Europe. As a side effect, moreover, free availability of imported goods, generally lower in price and higher in quality than competing domestic products, had the effect of building up a strong prejudice against local manufactures in general, which was partially and reluctantly overcome only when World War II and later import restrictions forced Argentine consumers to change their attitude.

The world depression hit Argentina by mid-1929. Economically, the depression directly affected exports and foreign investment, which represented the driving force of an economy which, as already mentioned, was directed towards the world market. By 1929, Argentina's agricultural production greatly exceeded domestic demand, while the nation's demand for capital goods, manufactured consumer goods, and fuels was far in excess of domestic production. The direct result of the decline in exports and the fall of world agricultural prices was a decline in the capacity to import. Consequently, an abrupt contraction was registered in aggregate domestic demand. The situation was worsened by the Ottawa Agreement of 1932, whereby Great Britain gave preferential treatment to the produce of the British Empire. Under such circumstances, the Conservative administration followed an economic policy which eventually prevented economic stagnation, a deterioration in the standard of living of the whole population, and widespread unemployment.

Selective controls were applied to the demand for imports by means of quantitative restrictions, a raise in tariffs, and the application of a system of multiple exchange rates. These measures naturally encouraged the development of those lines of production in which the disequilibrium between demand and domestic supply was most marked. Besides keeping national demand at high levels, the expansion of secondary industries was greatly stimulated. Many new industries came into existence, while the number of industrial establishments grew from 36,400 in 1933 to 44,300 in 1938 and 58,700 in 1944.[6] The growth of secondary industries was undoubtedly facilitated by the fact that large amounts had been invested in basic social capital before 1929, especially in the transportation sector, and by a relatively high rate of domestic saving — capital accumulated at a yearly rate of 1.4 per cent between 1925–29 and 1940–44, in spite of a net outflow of foreign capital. Furthermore, substitution of domestic manufactures for imports was made possible by the fact that Argentines had accumulated enough industrial experience during previous

[6] United Nations, *Processes and Problems of Industrialization in Under-Developed Countries*, New York, 1955, p. 133.

decades. But the fact that the Gross National Product remained at fairly high levels during the depression years and increased at a fair rate thereafter was fundamentally the result of governmental policies which permitted the expansion of the industrial sectors of the economy. Nevertheless, and in spite of their success in preventing the collapse of the Argentine economy during the depression years, the Conservatives have been severely — and perhaps not unjustly — criticized for their handling of the economy as a whole. Obviously, the main criticism applies to their farm policies.

The influence of landed interests in national life had not been seriously challenged through almost fourteen years (1916–1930) of Radical administration. The landowner kept real-estate taxes low, delayed the income tax until the 1930's, and kept it among the lowest in the world. Concentrated ownership of land was maintained even when dispersal of holdings was threatened by inheritance taxes: to avoid such duties (and income tax) landowners discovered the device of the company with anonymous shares. When laws were enacted to help small farmers buy land, they hindered implementation.[7] On the other hand, the world depression and the consequent fall of world prices for agricultural commodities inflicted a serious blow to Argentina's farming interests. Under such circumstances, the Ottawa Agreement, threatening to cause a reduction in the United Kingdom's demand for Argentine meat, caused serious alarm in Argentine landowning circles. Acting probably too hastily, the Conservative administration sent Vice-President Roca to London to negotiate with the British. Argentina's bargaining position was, of course, very weak. When, in May 1933, a trade treaty was finally signed — the so-called Roca-Runciman Treaty — it was attacked by almost everyone (the United States included) except the Argentine Conservatives and, of course, the British. According to the treaty, Great Britain would not reduce its imports of Argentine chilled beef in any quarter below a specified quantity. In return, Argentina reduced her tariffs on British goods, reserved the sterling earned from Argentine exports to the United Kingdom for remittance to Britain, converted blocked sterling funds into a 4 per cent sterling loan, and promised "benevolent treatment" and "legitimate protection" to British capitalists.[8] Obviously not without grounds, some of the provisions profoundly offended Argentine nationalists. And it increased the country's general dissatisfaction with its economic subservience to Great Britain. The treaty, however, helped to save the cattle industry and to secure foreign

[7] Hanson, S.: *op. cit.,* p. 88
[8] For a more extensive analysis of the treaty see Zymelman, M.: *op. cit.,* pp. 258–64; and Pendle: *op. cit.,* pp. 66–7.

exchange during a crucial period. By maintaining external demand at a relatively constant level, it also permitted further growth in agricultural production, necessary to satisfy increased domestic consumption.

Judged without bias, the conduct of economic affairs by the Conservative administrations through the 1930's must therefore be considered to have been passably good. The small increase achieved in per capita product was the most that could have been expected through a world depression which *forced* a complete redirection of the economy. Furthermore, while protecting farming activities, Argentina's prime source of foreign exchange, landowners did not interfere with industrial development, although they did not participate actively in the process. It is clear, however, that, a judgment as to the success or adequacy of their economic policies apart, through the 1930's as indeed since the very beginnings of Argentina's economic history, the ruling landowners steered Argentina's economy in accordance with — or so as to protect — their *personal* interests. Of course, we do not claim that international or domestic events of great scope and importance did not have definite influence upon the nation's economy in the short run. But we do contend that the general direction Argentina's economy was forced to take up to 1943 responded to the personality configuration — more specifically, to the value orientations — of the Argentine landowning class. Conclusive evidence to this effect was furnished in 1936, when the renegotiation of the Roca-Runciman Treaty produced an agreement even more unfavorable to Argentina than the original (1933) treaty:

> The harsh terms of the treaty were suprising in view of the fact that Argentina's bargaining power in 1936, with an export boom in process and world-wide prosperity, was much greater than in 1933, when the country was just emerging from the depth of the depression with a world situation that could not offer much relief and with the Ottawa Agreement hanging over Argentina's head. The treaty can be explained only as a sacrifice offered to protect the social and political status of the livestock group, a wish to maintain prosperity by insuring the principal market. . . . [9]

The reasons for this phenomenon should be clear at this point of our exposition. Cultural characteristics, typical of the national character, induce the Argentine:

(1) to put undue emphasis on personal, short-run advantage without adequate consideration of the future consequences that his actions may bring about for himself and the community;

(2) to respect and confer prestige to what is considered to be born

[9] Zymelman, M.: *op. cit.*, p. 264.

with the individual, and to assert it against other interests within the society as a right and a prerogative;

(3) to ignore self-doubts regarding the justification of his power and authority;

(4) to preserve at all costs what he has already gained or achieved for himself and his own family, and to value gains accrued to the community only insofar as he and his family are likely to profit from them;

(5) to blame other individuals or groups for the sorrowful consequences of his own acts.

All these cultural characteristics must have certainly compelled most individuals invested with political power (for many decades exclusively members of the old landowning aristocracy) consciously or unconsciously to direct the national economy so as to satisfy their own immediate interests. Unfortunately for the Argentine economy, never were such tendencies more pronounced than during the post-1943 era of dictatorship.

The Times of Dictatorship

The events which followed the 1943 military revolution cannot be clearly understood without first examining briefly Argentina's political structure.

The political history of the Republic can be best depicted in terms of the Argentine national character. It is a tale of power, of struggle between "superiors" and "subordinates," of autocracy, of complete centralization of decision-making in the hands of the ruling hierarchy — a natural consequence of the need dependency and need aggression conspicuous in the majority of Argentines. By and large, whoever has been in a position of political power has made use of it for his personal benefit. The nation's problems have been typically solved in terms of force and power — rarely by means of the co-operative, unselfish efforts of the individuals, communities, or institutions concerned. Revolution or public disorder has always been chosen as the best means to solve the problems of the nation; or to prevent serious national dislocations, real or imaginary. We must recognize, however, that solely by means of open rebellion have ideals and moral principles been able to prevail over the forces of dictatorship.

The first serious popular rebellion against the ruling Conservatives took place in July 1890. Although it was quickly suppressed, it nevertheless made clear that the fast-growing urban middle sectors could not forever be denied participation in the management of the Republic. It was not until 1912, however, that the Conservative-dominated Congress reluctantly enacted the so-called Sáenz Peña Law, providing for universal and compulsory male suffrage, the secret ballot, and minority representation in Congress. As was to be expected, thanks to this law the middle and lower sectors succeeded in electing their leader, Radical Hipólito Irigoyen, to the Presidency in the 1916 elections — thus terminating (at least for a while) the Conservative monopoly of government.

In many respects, Irigoyen's times presaged other, more difficult, years through which the nation was to live a generation later. Irigoyen, like Perón later, was the idol of the masses, the champion of the unprivileged. As President, he encouraged the rise of the middle sectors to positions of respectability; he even sponsored a number of mildly prolabor measures, an innovation in a country whose previous governments had given practically no consideration to labor questions; but he was not ready for the masses — or perhaps the masses were not yet ready for him. Encouraged by the fact that they enjoyed the President's sympathy, working elements typically chose the route of violence, disorder, and strikes to assert their rights. The events came to a climax in January 1919, when during the so-called *Semana Trágica* (the "Tragic Week"), the Buenos Aires police had to be instructed to stop by force the increasingly violent and numerous strikes. These clashes caused many deaths, and the mobs killed many more people. More importantly, these events were not the product of an organized popular movement. They were wild, uncontrolled outbursts of people who clamored for a voice in public affairs but who were neither educated nor culturally prepared to express their feelings as an organized entity or — let us put it this way — in a "civilized" manner. They followed the man, as they would later follow Perón, but the man did not supply them with a rallying social dogma, as did Perón. The Radical party was (and still is, much to the distress of its present leaders) a political rather than a labor movement. As such, it governed in terms of politics and politicians rather than social platforms and people. Under Irigoyen, the masses were never able to emerge as the predominant factor in society. In fact, at no point were the traditional patterns of political and economic organization seriously challenged. This may have prevented major economic setbacks.

Irigoyen was a stubborn believer in the democratic system of government. But, like every "true" Argentine — an individual with high need dependency and high need aggression — he was also an autocrat. He steadfastly refused to delegate authority and rarely trusted his subordinates — indeed, he became in his later years pathologically suspicious of everyone. Furthermore, although Irigoyen himself did not derive any personal benefit, there was inexperience, incompetence, and patent corruption in the conduct of public affairs. In spite of such obvious defects, the Argentine electorate chose Radical Alvear in 1922 and re-elected the already senile Irigoyen in 1928 to the Presidency.[10] Presidential leadership after 1928 was almost nonexistent, and Irigoyen was thus completely unable to cope with problems associated with the Great Depression. For all practical purposes, the constitutional government had ceased to exist before it was formally deposed by a military, Conservative-inspired revolt on September 6, 1930.

Wide discontent on account of unemployment and the threat of fore-closure of farmers' mortgages gave to the Conservative revolution an appearance of popular support it did not truly deserve. In fact, the new *de facto* President declared in December 1930 that the Sáenz Peña Law was a pernicious piece of legislation, that the democratic system was evil, and that government should be conducted by an élite, a selected minority within the country.[11] Although, under the pressure of public opinion, the revolution called for Presidential elections in 1931, these elections and the ones which followed in 1938 were conducted with manipulations openly labeled by the Conservatives as a "patriotic fraud." Government-supported candidates won both the 1931 and 1938 elections. The control of government was thus restored to the old landed élite. The experience of the twenties should have made them realize that "new winds were blowing over the pampas," that they could not forever deny all other sectors of the population an active voice in the affairs of the Republic, and that serious dislocations would occur in the event of a seizure of power by the politically uneducated masses. Those in control of the government, however, not only denied democracy to the people but also refused to acknowledge the fact that basic changes had occurred in the sources of the nation's wealth.

Around 1944, the net value of manufacturing output surpassed the net value of agricultural and livestock production. More people were employed in industry than on the farms. Economic power was rapidly moving into different hands, a situation which sooner or later was bound to reflect itself in the political arena.[12] Nevertheless, the landowning élite stubbornly clung to traditional patterns of social, political, and economic organization. Why? Certainly not out of greed, avarice, lack of patriotism, or other such peculiarities, of which they were later accused by the dictatorship's propaganda machinery. Murena saw "a pride which wore

[10] Irigoyen was barred by the Constitution from succeeding himself. In English, more can be read about these topics in Pendle: *op. cit.;* and Whitaker, A.: *The United States and Argentina* (Cambridge, Mass., Harvard University Press, 1954).

[11] See also Blanksten, G.: *Peron's Argentina* (Chicago, The University of Chicago Press, 1953), p. 36.

[12] See also United Nations, C.E.P.A.L.: *El Desarrollo Económico de la Argentina*, Part I, p. 116; and Pendle: *op. cit.*, p. 75.

the mask of beneficent 'patriarchalism' " as the main cause.[13] We of course insist that the basic reason must be found in the Argentine national character.

Similarly, we maintain that the fundamental causes of Argentina's economic collapse under Perón have been *social* and not economic, as it is widely assumed. Many Argentines still believe that Perón's dictatorship was a matter of "luck"; that following the 1943 Fascist-military revolt, the emergence of Perón as a leader of the masses was a turn of the wheels of fortune, which could have brought order and progress as readily as demagoguery and economic stagnation. Nothing, we believe, could be more erroneous — or more in accordance with the Argentine's value orientations. Given Argentina's value-orientation profile and the resulting socio-political organization of the nation, the re-emergence of a force akin to Sarmiento's "barbarism" as the major element in society was sooner or later inevitable. The process by which it came into being will be discussed in connection with our analysis of Argentine labor in Chapter 5. It is, however, important to stress now some of the consequences of this phenomenon. During at least ten years (1945–1955), Argentina witnessed the rule of corruption, mediocrity, force, selfishness, disorder, hate, disunity — in one word, "barbarism" — in all sectors of the society's life. We believe that any economic policy Perón might have chosen to follow — whether more or less disastrous, from a purely academic point of view, than the ones he actually pursued — would have led the country to the same ultimate result. (We shall see, however, that Perón's policies were largely *conditioned* by his cultural tendencies.) The real, fundamental problem did not lie in the nature and number of the more or less important, domestic or international, economic difficulties the dictatorship had to face. Far more basic was the fact that the Argentine society was by no means prepared to solve constructively *any kind of problem* within the scope, and to the benefit of, its institutions, the community, or indeed the social order. Otherwise, it would seem absolutely inexplicable that Argentina, a country which had handsomely weathered great international dislocations such as two world wars and a world depression, could have collapsed economically through a decade of almost unprecedented economic advance throughout the whole world.

At the end of World War II, Argentina "had come to be in the position of a large enterprise which has working capital at its disposal but lacks resources to finance its expansion." [14] Its population was almost 40 per cent larger, its Gross National Product roughly 40 per cent larger,

[13] As quoted in Hanke, L.: *South America* (Princeton, N. J., D. Van Nostrand Co., 1959), p. 161.
[14] United Nations, C.E.P.A.L.: *Economic Bulletin for Latin America,* Vol. IV, No. 1, p. 15.

its industrial production 65 per cent higher than around 1930. But exports, which represented 21.9 per cent of Gross National Product in 1930–34, had declined to 19.1 per cent and 13.0 per cent of Gross National Product in 1935–39 and 1940–44, respectively.[15] As a result, the nation found itself by 1945 without enough foreign exchange to finance the imports of capital goods it needed to raise its per capita product significantly, although its foreign-exchange position sufficed to maintain fairly constant levels of activity.

The situation was complemented by other factors. First, the expansion of secondary industries during the preceding periods made it practically impossible to free additional foreign exchange through an import substitution process in the field of consumer goods. Second, it was essential to the nation's progress that large sums of capital be invested in the transportation sectors, where necessary expansion and adequate replacements had been delayed since the 1920's. Third, large investments were also necessary in the agricultural sector. While agricultural production had been able to keep pace with the growth of population during the 1940's, peace in Europe and a pronounced increase in the rate of population growth (accentuated after 1947 by the arrival of new immigration waves) made an increase in agricultural production imperative. With the possibilities of expansion through the incorporation of new land exhausted since the beginning of the twenties, increased production could only have been achieved through increased productivity. This of course would have demanded large investments. Finally, the rapid development of industry and motorized transportation during the thirties and early forties caused a marked increase in demand for fuels, especially petroleum. Efforts to keep down petroleum prices after 1945 accelerated the growth of demand and restricted those financial means necessary to expand domestic supply at least at a corresponding rate.[16]

If, at that time, market forces had been allowed free play and no attempt whatsoever had been made to offset their effects, serious economic dislocations might have developed. Some measure of restriction, of governmental redirection of the economy, was needed to encourage balanced growth (the expansion of farming activities to reverse the trend of steadily declining exports observed during and after the war; and simultaneous substitution of imports in capital goods, fuels, and other intermediate products). A restricted measure of honest, competent, state control over the economy was indeed essential.

Instead, and under the (by itself acceptable) banner of industrialization as a primary national objective, the dictatorship systematized and widely

---

[15] *Ibid.*, p. 15; and United Nations, C.E.P.A.L.: *El Desarrollo. . . ,* p. 18.
[16] United Nations, C.E.P.A.L.: *Economic Bulletin . . . ,* pp. 15–16.

extended existing measures, and devised new schemes, of governmental control. The aim was economic self-sufficiency for Argentina, which is of course largely utopian but the enunciation of which has a powerful propaganda value. The actual result was economic collapse.

In accordance with his (culturally patterned) autocratic tendencies, Perón set up a series of agencies to take over all sections of the economy.[17] Foremost among them was the so-called IAPI (Argentine Institute for the Promotion of Trade), created in 1946. This agency was given the right to buy virtually the whole of Argentina's agricultural and livestock production and to sell it wherever the best price could be obtained. By paying low prices to local producers and obtaining high prices from foreign buyers, it realized huge profits, which were utilized partly to import goods that would have ranked very low on a satisfactory list of priorities (American war surplus, for instance), partly to support the propaganda machinery of the government or to gain personal enrichment for the *peronista* hierarchy. The institute was also the chief instrument through which a policy of redistributing income in favor of the urban population was followed. This was achieved through the maintenance of low relative prices for agricultural commodities, and direct consumer subsidies. These and additional measures — such as the freezing of both urban and farm rents — did little to attract investors towards agriculture.

Together with the creation of IAPI, nationalization of the Central Bank (which had been founded by the Conservatives in 1934) assured the state control of the nation's basic financial and economic processes. Further, the new Constitution enacted in 1949 enunciated the principle of state ownership of the natural and power resources of the country. And foreign-exchange reserves were utilized to nationalize foreign investments (the railroads, the telephone system, port facilities, grain elevators, mines, etc.). As has been mentioned earlier in this book, the nationalization spree which swept the country during the forties, as well as the inclusion in the Argentine industrialization program of such projects as an atomic energy plant, the production of heavy military craft, and the like, can be ultimately accounted for in terms of the society's — and, therefore, its leader's — unconscious drive to achieve power and greatness without adjusting to, or "paying the consequences" of, the psychological and social transformations necessary to build a modern industrial society. At any rate, the *economic* yield of the nationalization of foreign investments was far lower than the benefits which would have accrued to the country had foreign-exchange reserves been utilized for investments in transportation, energy (especially petroleum), and necessary capital-

[17] See also Pendle, G.: *op. cit.,* p. 89; and Whitaker, A.: *op. cit.,* pp. 177–185.

goods industries. Actually, the rate of capital formation in these latter sectors was grossly inadequate. Only those industries manufacturing consumer goods showed an acceptable — if not sufficient — rate of capital formation between 1940–44 and 1955. But as much as 73.9 per cent of the capital accumulated by the nation during that period was diverted to sectors of the economy that were not directly productive: housing, service industries, and, foremost, the immense bureaucratic machinery of the state.[18]

The defective distribution of investments produced most harmful effects on the distribution of the working population among the various types of employment. Although more will be said about this topic when we discuss the productivity of the Argentine labor force in Chapter 5, we should note here that the ratio of industrial manpower to total economically active population *decreased* between 1940–44 and 1955, a drastic reversal of the trend observed in previous decades. Accordingly, the very high annual rate of growth in industrial employment registered during the period 1935–45 (7.4 per cent annually) went down to 1.7 per cent annually from 1945 to 1947. And between 1948 and 1955, industrial employment generally decreased from year to year. In particular, manufacturing employment declined 11 per cent between 1948 and 1954 (while the nation's general level of employment remained at fairly constant levels).[19] At least since 1948, therefore, the industrialization program launched by Perón did not fulfill an indispensable dynamic function: the gradual and continuous increase of the proportion of total manpower engaged in industrial activities. This fact, together with the other aspects of the economic process sketched in preceding paragraphs, shows that contrary to the indictment of overindustrialization sustained by certain sectors of the Argentine public opinion, industry did not develop sufficiently, or in appropriate fields, during Perón's era.

SINCE 1955

When, by 1955, the dictatorship was finally overthrown by the Army, Perón's economic policies had left the country virtually bankrupt. Despite the emphasis on industrialization, per capita production had increased only 3.5 per cent since 1945. Exports were 50 per cent below the

[18] United Nations, C.E.P.A.L.: *El Desarrollo* . . . , pp. 20–36.

[19] *Ibid.*, pp. 36–41; United Nations: *Report on the World Social Situation* (New York, 1957), p. 98; and U. S. Department of Labor, Bureau of Labor Statistics: *Foreign Labor Information — Labor in Argentina* (Washington, D. C., 1959), p. 3. All employment figures include only wage earners (thus excluding salaried employees). "Industrial employment" includes employment in manufacturing, extractive, electrical, and gas industries.

levels of pre-World War II years. Hence, the supply of capital goods was seriously curtailed. Compared with prewar levels, the planted wheat acreage was down by almost one-third, corn by one-half, and flaxseed by three-fourths. The net gold and foreign-exchange reserves held by the Central Bank, amounting to 5,646 million pesos in 1947, dwindled to 1,485 million pesos in 1955. Efforts to redistribute income in favor of the urban areas and, at the same time, an incompatible effort to maintain the level of investment led inevitably to wild inflation: the supply of money in circulation, which totaled 8 billion pesos in 1945, reached 60 billion pesos in 1955.[20]

The Army officers who overthrew Perón in 1955 were perfectly aware of the economic debacle at hand, but their main goal was to surrender power peacefully to civilian elements by means of honest elections. Although they clearly aimed at a return to private enterprise, a radical departure from governmental control would have been hardly feasible, given Perón's institutional legacy. Nevertheless, serious efforts were made to improve the investment climate, unrestricted capital movements were permitted, the exchange system was simplified, banking was decentralized, artificial trade barriers were reduced, the IAPI was abolished, and efforts were made to revive agriculture. Basically sound economic policies, however, failed to start a long-overdue recovery. By 1957, per capita Gross National Product was 1.1 per cent lower, per capita gross income 2.7 per cent lower than corresponding 1955 levels.[21]

The situation quickly worsened after Dr. Frondizi assumed the Presidency in May 1958. Overwhelmingly elected by a coalition of dissident Radicals, Peronists, and Communists, the new administration was firmly committed through campaign promises to policies that were in most respects at least as nationalistic as those pursued by Perón. President Frondizi, however, has had the courage and good sense to change his original ideas. On December 29, 1958, he announced drastic measures to save the country from economic ruin.[22] With inflation completely out of control, he launched an austerity program aimed at stabilization and economic development. Credits were restricted, government expenditures drastically cut, and foreign investments encouraged. Substantial loans were negotiated with European and U.S. banks and the International Monetary Fund. Under newly signed contracts with United States and European companies, intensive — and long-overdue — oil exploitation has been undertaken. As a consequence, oil imports, which were the major cause of a crippling trade deficit, dropped from 280

[20] U. S. Department of Labor: *op. cit.*, p. 2.
[21] United Nations, C.E.P.A.L., *El Desarrollo.* . . . , p. 15.
[22] His message has been partially reprinted in Hanke, L.: *op. cit.*, pp. 162–165.

million dollars in 1957 to 174 million dollars in 1959 and should cease by 1961, thus freeing sorely needed foreign exchange.[23] Furthermore, the present government seems to regard massive industrialization as the remedy for all illnesses which have plagued the country since the mid-1940's.

Although the economy has been stabilized and the inflationary process largely tamed, it is too soon to judge whether economic recovery is yet under way. For one thing, the social and political climate remains turbulent and highly unstable, with periodic threats of armed rebellion, terrorism, labor disturbances, frequent strikes, and the like. We personally believe that a process of steady recovery of the nation's economy has not yet begun. More importantly, very few responsible Argentine and foreign economists expect a definite measure of recovery for some years to come. Eventually, theoreticians may begin to realize that the fundamental causes of Argentina's economic stagnation are of a social character, rather than purely economic.

It is, however, important to stress that the responsibility for this situation — as well as for the political and economic events which led to it — cannot be exclusively imputed to one individual, a political party, or a social class. Quite possibly, nobody is or has been responsible for it, since it seems to have been the outcome of an inevitable social process. But at the same time everybody is responsible. It has been and it is the problem of all individuals and all classes because all have contributed to it and all have failed to solve it. It is the problem of the Argentine; of his "basic personality"; of the value-orientation profile of an abstract, inorganic society.

The last word in the struggle between "civilization" and "barbarism" may not have been said yet. One is compelled to believe that unless the conflicting forces within the Argentine society are somehow reconciled, the nation's development will continue to be a succession of ups and downs, depending on which leader brings what force at what time to the dominant position, and regardless of the course Argentina's economy may be forced to take by such a leader. Briefly, and to the point, we believe that steady, long-run economic development will hardly take place in Argentina unless there is a simultaneous change in the value-orientation profile of the society.

Of course, to adopt now a negative position and conclude that, after all, steady economic development is not possible in Argentina would be equally indefensible. The analysis of the Argentine national character has been undertaken because by discovering and understanding the causes of its weaknesses and defects (from an economic-development

---

[23] *Time*, December 21, 1959, p. 25.

standpoint), we will be in a much better position to offer a constructive suggestion as to *what should be done* in order to insure the success of present or future economic-development programs. We will suggest in our concluding chapter that it is in the field of industrial relations where a progressive development of the society's value-orientation profile towards higher degrees of "activity" can and must be initiated. In order to better understand such problems, however, we must first turn to a brief survey of today's industrial relations in general and of Argentine industrial management and the Argentine labor force in particular.

4 INDUSTRIAL MANAGEMENT IN ARGENTINA

I N THIS chapter, we shall be chiefly interested in Argentine management "as a system of authority." [1] Although the prevailing system is, by the force of post-1943 events, the constitutional type of management, we may safely assert that within such limits most characteristics of authoritarian, paternalistic, and (at least recently in state enterprises) participative managements can also be found in Argentine enterprises. What we will describe here is management as it is usually found in private industrial enterprises. But we must keep in mind that from the point of view of its structure, practices, training, education, political ideology, economic strength, and philosophy towards labor and business in general, the Argentine "managerial class" constitutes anything but a compact, uniform group. [2]

MANAGERIAL FUNCTIONS

Before undertaking the discussion of some of management's shortcomings, it seems appropriate to devote a few paragraphs to the defense (or at least the interpretation) of some of management's most criticized ways and means.

Argentine entrepreneurs have been widely criticized for their tendencies toward cartelization, monopolies, nepotism, and in general, concentration of ownership. They have also been critically judged for their unwillingness to take risks and reinvest earnings "productively," and for

[1] The terminology used in this chapter follows the one introduced by Harbison, F., and Myers, C. A., in *Management in the Industrial World* (New York, McGraw-Hill, 1959), Part I.

[2] Unfortunately, there are (to our knowledge) no published studies of Argentine industrial management, its problems or practices. Part of the analysis that follows will therefore rely exclusively on personal experiences, observations, and opinions. Therefore, the reader should probably allow for some margin of error owing to incomplete information and biased appreciation of the reality.

their prevailing philosophy of high profits per unit of sale rather than mass markets at low unit profits. These criticisms are all valid, well-founded, and obviously constructive from an economic-development point of view. But such practices have not come about by the joint and purposed decision of interested businessmen. They are the automatic response to largely identifiable causes. And as long as these *causes* do not disappear, their effects may not be easily corrected.

The "high profits per unit" philosophy has been unquestionably nourished by the protectionist policies followed by Argentine governments since the mid-1930's. Protectionism breeds and will continue to breed inefficiency. Barred from the influence of foreign competition, Argentine industry has been able to pass on to the consumer the increased costs of governmental labor policies and has adapted itself comfortably to producing large profits on the smallest possible volume. It is no exaggeration to state that most Argentine industrialists regard with panic the possibility of a relaxation of tariff barriers and other protectionist measures. Many industries would soon go out of existence if certain foreign goods were allowed to be imported. For many industries, the stage of justified protectionism under the "infant industry" argument lies already in the remote past. The "high profits per unit" philosophy is only one of the many prices Argentine industry is paying for an administratively ill-conceived industrialization process. We must also keep in mind, however, that such an approach to profits is partly the consequence of a "trader" business mentality not unrelated to cultural characteristics which induce the Argentine to maximize his immediate advantage (in this case the business' short-run profits), while neglecting adequate consideration of future goals and long-run profitability. Furthermore, the "mass markets at low unit profits" philosophy is only possible where a mass market exists at all. For most durables and many consumer products, this is not the case in Argentina. Argentines may have been educated to middle-class appetites, but certainly only a few have middle-class incomes.

Clearly, the possibility of unpredictable and arbitrary government action, always latent in Argentina's business world, greatly enhances investment risks. Furthermore, Argentine entrepreneurs are often required to make decisions — with regard to production techniques, scale of operation, location of factory, means of distribution, and so on — without any accurate knowledge of some of the key variables which will undoubtedly affect the result of their investment and with only restricted access to specialized institutions capable of relieving the entrepreneur of part of the burden. The incentives to save or expand into new fields are few, living as the Argentine businessman does in a world of continuing inflation. It is obvious that the most practical course for him to take to insure himself against losses from monetary devaluation is to invest his savings "unproductively" in real estate and long-term foreign investments, or to resort to immediate luxury consumption. And since the risk of "productive" investments is great, interest rates are extremely high (reflecting also the pressure of demand for capital on available funds). High interest rates are unquestionably a deterrent to investment, especially in industries requiring a large initial investment and long years of development before profits appear. Thus the vicious circle is closed. The latter situation is also attributable to the fact that many industrialists have commerce, banking, moneylending, or real-estate backgrounds and often tend to take a speculative rather than an investment view of capital expenditure, laying primary stress on immediate returns rather than on the long-term growth of the enterprise.

Argentine entrepreneurs have been also criticized for managing their enterprises by following a "rule-of-thumb" method rather than orthodox "profit maximization" strategies. There is no doubt that Argentine managers are far from having adequate knowledge of modern administrative tools and methods. Managerial efficiency could indeed be greatly increased if serious management-development programs were undertaken. On the other hand, there are also personality factors which help to explain this tendency. As a result of their value orientations, entrepreneurs tend to subordinate pure business ends and material goals to prestige, family, or friendship considerations. Usually the profit motive, far from being the sole determining factor, is only a guiding element in managerial decisions. Very often, "the executive first plans what *ought* to be done and then plans as best he can *to make his action pay*." [3]

Finally, managerial efficiency is seriously impaired by lack of competition in industry. Generally, Argentines do not feel the kind of antagonism towards monopolies and cartels conspicuous in U.S. public opinion. Their opposition to trusts in general is the consequence of, and applies only to, the exploitation of industry by foreign interests and their power in world markets; only rarely does it stem from profound convictions in the free-enterprise system. There is therefore a high degree of concentration of ownership in privately controlled industries.

THE STRUCTURE OF MANAGEMENT

Argentine industry is currently facing the usual problems inherent in a transition from personal to functional management. As has already

---

[3] Whyte, W., and Holmberg, A.: *Human Problems of U. S. Enterprise in Latin America, 1956* (Ithaca, N. Y., New York State School of Industrial and Labor Relations, Cornell University), p. 10. (Italics in the original.)

been mentioned, national industrial establishments are largely the product of immigrant entrepreneurship. Throughout the beginnings of industrialization, although certain phases of commerce and industry were nearly monopolized by foreign capital, there were enough opportunities for enterprising immigrants and some natives to share directly in the process of industrial growth. Their establishments were naturally small in scale and organized as individual ventures, partnerships, or at best family-owned enterprises. Such individuals usually came from non-industrial occupations, but at least the eventually successful ones must have been equipped with ambitions and energy of an unusual kind in order to be able to overcome their lack of knowledge of industrial problems and the absence of natives trained in industrial and administrative skills. For the same reasons, the new entrepreneurs must have had to assume a variety of managerial functions, thus setting the cornerstone for a (still widespread) pattern of organization built upon close personal control.

As the industrialization process advanced, however, many undertakings reached a point where it was no longer possible for a single individual to take care of the expanding operations. At the first stage, this led to the organization of "patrimonial" undertakings, based on the head of family's cultural obligation to provide employment and adequate income and status for the various members of his immediate and extended family. In the course of time, however, family control has sometimes tended to weaken as a result of the division of ownership interests through inheritance, further growth of operations, and the absence of the founder's drive, energy, and vision. Slowly, nepotism has had to give way to the need for professional management, first at the lower, then at higher, managerial ranks. Thus, in large enterprises it is not uncommon to find top-management levels staffed with members of the original founder's family, while lower executive ranks are largely filled by professional managers. The emergence of a professional "managerial class" in industry has also been fostered since the 1940's by the participation of government in the economic field. Many professionals with commercial, financial, engineering, or law backgrounds have been given the opportunity to reach top-management positions in large state enterprises—an opportunity they would have been less likely to find in private, family-owned establishments.

In those enterprises where time and growth have forced the abandonment of the "one-man rule" type of management, the functions of the board of directors tend to be of much wider scope than in the United States, for instance. In large Argentine enterprises, it is not unusual for a board to supervise in detail all operations of the firm. This is but one example of a feature, conspicuous through all levels of management, which has been examined at length elsewhere in this book: the culturally patterned reluctance to delegate authority and responsibilities. It is, however, important to note that from an organizational point of view, overcentralization of authority has serious consequences; to the detriment of the indispensable training and development of lower managerial cadres and of the over-all efficiency of the enterprise, the functional responsibilities of middle and lower management tend to be only vaguely defined. This results in frequent overlapping of duties and responsibilities (which means that more often than not these are not carried out) or in the total neglect of functions to which nobody in the organization has been specifically assigned. Obviously, such personnel lack incentives to better their performance. This is especially the case when, in addition to the monotony of a job with little responsibility, the "road upward" is blocked by family barriers. At best, such people may look at their jobs as a mere foothold from which to launch their own (small-scale) business careers. Real identification with the purposes and goals of the organization is rare, a phenomenon which is also perfectly understandable in terms of the Argentine's basic Being-orientation.

Argentine industry draws heavily from the professions (mainly engineers) to fill managerial, administrative, and supervisory positions. This feature is of course not unrelated to the fact that professional life has a prestige well above that of business and industry. The ambitious young Argentine will therefore typically choose an academic career as the best means to achieve social recognition. The supply of professionals, however, far exceeds the demand for their specific talents. Naturally, business and industry supply the materially most interesting alternative. As a rule, however, professional men have only a rudimentary knowledge of management methods and techniques. Although a few management courses for engineering students are offered at some universities, these courses very often barely cover minimum requirements.[4]

Finally, another serious deficiency of Argentine industry is the shortage of competent foremen. This is not so much the consequence of a lack of technically skilled or adequately trained personnel as, at least since the 1940's, a matter of lack of incentives. Pay differences between foremen and workers have been systematically reduced (by legislation or contractual arrangements) in most industries. This situation is especially unfortunate because foremen were usually recruited from middle-income families and were thus used to higher living standards than most workers. The deterioration of their purchasing power since the early 1950's has been therefore

---

[4] The recent decision of the University of Buenos Aires to establish a School of Business Administration is an encouraging new development, as is the growth of private management training institutes within the last few years.

doubly frustrating.[5] Furthermore, in many trades foremen lost during the Perón dictatorship much of their prestige by being forced to join production workers' unions. Although joint unionization was prohibited in 1956 by governmental decree, much of the authority lost during those years has been difficult to regain in practice.

GOVERNMENT INFLUENCE ON INDUSTRIAL RELATIONS

The state has increasingly intervened in the development of industry since World War II. In few areas has this intervention assumed greater proportions than in the field of industrial relations. The role of government has not been circumscribed to the enactment of labor legislation and the encouragement of the growth of trade unions. It has also established procedures and created administrative organs for the handling of labor-management relations at the national, industry-wide, or plant levels.[6]

Labor Legislation

Argentina has no single labor code. The nation's labor legislation, therefore, is a loose accumulation of Constitutional dispositions, legislative decrees, court interpretations, and collective-bargaining clauses. Basic to the matter of labor and social rights is an amendment to the 1853 Constitution of the Argentine Republic, approved by the National Constitutional Convention in October 1957. A new article was inserted in the Constitution stating, among other provisions, that

> Labor in its various forms shall be protected by laws guaranteeing every employee decent and equitable conditions of employment, fixed hours of work, rest periods and leave with pay, fair remuneration, an adjustable minimum living wage, equal pay for equal work, *a share in the profits made by undertakings, with a right to participate in management and in the organization of production,* protection against arbitrary dismissal, stability of employment in the public service, and the free and democratic organization of trade unions, which shall be recognized by the mere fact of their being entered in a special register.
>
> Trade unions shall be guaranteed the right to conclude collective labor

[5] See also República Argentina, Dirección Nacional de Industrias del Estado (DiNIE): *Reseña de las Actividades del Organismo* (Buenos Aires, Ministerio de Industria y Comercio de la Nación, 1958), pp. 57–63.

[6] For a more detailed analysis of these topics, see Fillol, T.: *Industrial Relations in the Economic Development of Argentina,* unpublished S.M. thesis (Massachusetts Institute of Technology, 1960), pp. 59–126; and U. S. Department of Labor, Bureau of Labor Statistics: *Foreign Labor Information — Labor in Argentina* (Washington, D. C., June 1959). In the following pages, we will present a brief summary of Argentine labor legislation, social-security schemes, and labor relations in order to emphasize the importance of the role played by the state in influencing industrial relations.

agreements, the right to resort to conciliation and arbitration and the right to strike. . . .

The State shall award benefits under the social security scheme, which shall be comprehensive and obligatory. . . . [7]

This amendment reflects the climate of political campaigning in which the sessions of the Constitutional Convention were held. It represents, however, the first *significant* enunciation of labor rights in the text of an Argentine Constitution. The one enacted in 1853, being frankly liberal and written at a time when Argentina was little more than a collection of small warring provinces, did not contain any principles of social legislation, but its ample clauses permitted the gradual creation of a body of labor laws through legislative action. Perón's 1949 Constitution (later declared null by the 1955 Revolutionary government) included sections in which broad social principles were enunciated — foremost among them, the so-called "Rights of the Worker." These principles, however, were nothing but another pompous and meaningless piece of propaganda. [8]

Since 1943 Argentina has to a great extent abandoned labor legislation by trades, occupation, or industry. Most of the laws enacted and decrees issued since then concern the whole of the labor force. Today, Argentine labor legislation provides for: maximum working hours (both for day and night work, and for work in unhealthful occupations); weekly rest periods, including Saturday half-day rest (a law which effectively institutes the 44-hour week for workers and employees in commerce and industry); paid national holidays and other nonworking days, and the amount of pay for any time worked during such days; annual paid vacations; protection of women and minors (establishing minimum legal work ages, hours of work, special rest periods, maternal care and services, etc.); a national minimum wage (first established in 1956); an obligatory annual bonus (*aguinaldo*, or thirteenth-month pay); family allowances (introduced in 1957); etc. Perón introduced the *aguinaldo* and adjusted some of the above-mentioned labor standards. Apart from these few cases, however, all labor standards are either of pre-1943, or recent post-1955, date.

In addition to wage supplements provided by the law, most workers receive benefits over and above wages under the terms of collective agreements. These commonly include benefits such as: a fixed number of days' leave with pay, and payment of subsidies, for family affairs such as births, weddings, and burials; compensation for workers in military service; monthly allowances for married workers and for disabled dependent rela-

[7] International Labour Office: *Legislative Series, 1957 — Argentina* 2 (Geneva. January–February 1959). (Italics added.)
[8] This point is elaborated in Fillol, T.: *op. cit.*, pp. 79–82.

tives; etc. Since workers and employees are also entitled by law to a fixed number of paid days of vacation and since they also receive pay for time lost because of illness or injury, a worker may expect, all legal and contractually specified benefits added, to receive supplementary earnings equivalent to an average of about 30 per cent of his basic wage.[9]

Social Security

Practically all active Argentines over eighteen years of age (including self-employed workers, employers, and members of the professions) are today covered by old-age, disability, and survivors-insurance programs. Commercial and industrial pension funds usually come from contributions of 25 per cent of total wages and salaries — 10 per cent from the employee and 15 per cent from the employer. Pension benefits are based upon the wages currently in force and not upon those which the pensioner received when in employment. In other words, pensions are linked with the cost of living. Furthermore, pensions are calculated in relation to total earnings (basic wage or salary plus bonuses, thirteenth-month pay, etc.). The average pensioner receives annually about 82 per cent of his or her average earnings for the five years (which may not be consecutive) of highest earnings, adjusted to current standards.

Legislation covering industrial accidents, occupational diseases, and compensation for them makes every employer liable for the accidents sustained by his salaried or wage-earning employees during their employment or on the journey between the workplace and the home of the worker, unless the accident is intentionally brought about by the injured person or where it is due to *force majeure* unconnected with the work. Similar dispositions make the employer liable for workers' occupational diseases. Employers are required to provide medical, surgical, hospital, and pharmaceutical services; such prosthetic and orthopedic appliances as are considered necessary; funeral expenses where the accident or disease has caused the worker's death; and payments to the worker or his surviving dependents according to a fixed scale of compensation. The government provides for maternity benefits through the Maternity Fund, to which each female worker between the ages of fifteen and forty-five contributes the equivalent of one day's pay per quarter. Equal sums are paid to the fund by the employer and by government.

[9] U. S. Department of Labor: *op. cit.*, p. 20. A detailed analysis of the supplementary benefits accorded by collective agreements in force during 1956–57 has been published by C. Belaúnde: *Los Convenios Colectivos de Trabajo en la Argentina* (Buenos Aires, Selección Contable, 1958). See also Fillol: *op. cit.*, pp 89–90. In Argentina, common usage generally differentiates salaried (white-collar) *employees* from wage-earning (blue-collar) *workers*. In general, in this monograph we do *not* abide by the same rule; that is, we will often use the terms "employee" and "worker" interchangeably.

A basic principle of Argentine labor law is the worker's right to his job. This principle is contained in Act No. 11,729 (1934). Although its provisions deal mainly with the determination of the employment relationship of commercial employees, court decisions have extended the coverage of the act's dismissal-procedures provisions to industrial workers as well.[10]

Employers are in principle free to dismiss any of their workers provided that they comply with two main obligations: *advance notice* and payment of a *severance allowance*. Unless a longer period is fixed by agreement between the parties, the period of notice of dismissal is one month if the length of service is less than five years, or two months if it is more than five years. In all cases of dismissal without "just cause," the minimum obligatory severance payment to the dismissed worker or employee is one month's remuneration for each year of service or part of a year exceeding three months.

In case of dismissal for "just cause," the employer need not observe a period of notice nor pay severance allowance. According to rules and principles developed by legislation and the courts, "just cause" covers such things as infractions of discipline, negligence, disobedience, misconduct, long and repeated absenteeism, failure to observe the time schedule, and the like. If the dismissal is the result of justifiable "reduction or lack of work," an amendment (1945) to the 1934 act stipulates explicitly that employees are entitled to an indemnity, the amount of which is 50 per cent of the severance allowance in general cases. According to the same amendment, an employer may also "suspend" (and not dismiss) the employee for economic (lack of work) reasons. The maximum period of suspension is thirty days (although it may be extended to 90 days in cases of *force majeure*) at the end of which an employee may consider himself as dismissed, entitling him to full severance allowance. "Suspension" temporarily relieves the employee of his obligation to be at the disposal of the employer, and the employer of his obligation to pay the wage or salary.

According to the 1934 act, an employee whose work is interrupted by a nonoccupational illness or accident for which he is not to blame is not only entitled to his full remuneration during such interruption for a certain maximum period (six months after ten years of service, three months after less than ten years) but he also retains a right to his job for one year after the time limit of three or six months. If the employer dismisses the employee during this one-year period, he must pay the normal severance allowance.

Dismissal or suspension of an employee for the purpose of impeding

[10] Krotoschin, E.: *Tratado Práctico de Derecho del Trabajo,* Vol. I (Buenos Aires, Ed. Depalma, 1955), p. 68. The following analysis of job security in Argentina is based on *International Labour Review,* Vol. LXXX, No. 6 (December 1959), pp. 520–527.

his exercise of trade-union rights would constitute an unfair labor practice according to Act. No. 14,455 of August 1958. An employee holding a trade-union office or having similar functions as a workers' representative, a member of a works committee or of another industrial representative body enjoys job security. If, on assuming one of these offices or functions, he is unable to continue working, employers are required to hold the employee's position open for him, to reinstate him on the expiration of his term of function or office, and not to discharge him without "just cause" for one year thereafter.

Labor-Management Relations

The state has also made certain voluntary forms of handling labor-management relations to a great extent unnecessary. Thus, legislation has been enacted, or decrees issued, governing the negotiation and scope of collective agreements, establishing the procedure to be followed in handling collective disputes, and regulating strikes and lockouts.

Although the first *collective agreement* was signed in Argentina in 1901,[11] only under Perón did it become regular practice to negotiate national collective agreements covering entire industries. Before 1943, the usual practice was the contract between employer and each individual worker or employee. Only in very few industries had collective agreements ever been signed, and these were regulated by clauses included in differential legislation applying to particular trades or occupations.[12] After 1943, an industry-wide approach to collective bargaining was encouraged not only by the formation of powerful trade-unions, but also by the bestowal, in 1953, of legal status upon an officially sponsored, nation-wide association of employers, the General Economic Confederation (C.G.E.). Perón's intention was to concentrate in the C.G.E. the monopoly on collective bargaining for employers, in order to have the latter more directly under governmental control, and also in order to build a strong counterpart to the General Confederation of Labor (C.G.T.). In effect, between 1953 and 1956, a law required that collective bargaining be conducted by employers' and workers' federations with incorporated status. Although this law (which is no longer in force) allowed employers, under certain circumstances, to form *ad hoc* representative bodies and even to participate in an individual capacity, industry-wide collective bargaining has been securely established in Argentina.[13]

Practically all workers and employees are covered today by collective

[11] Vernengo, R.: "Freedom of Association and Industrial Relations in Latin America; Part II," in *International Labour Review*, Vol. LXXIII, No. 6 (June 1956) p. 594 n.

[12] See also Garzón Ferreyra, I.: *La Convención Colectiva de Trabajo* (Buenos Aires, Ed. Arayú, 1954), pp. 37–40; and Belaúnde, C.: *op. cit.*, pp. 5–8.

[13] U. S. Dept. of Labor: *op. cit.*, p. 12; and Vernengo, R.: *op. cit.*, p. 597.

agreements. Legislation covering such agreements was first enacted in September 1953 (Act. No. 14,250). This means that during at least eight years of widespread use, application and enforcement of collective agreements were subject to the interpretation of the courts or, more often, of the Ministry of Labor and Welfare. This obviously facilitated governmental settlement of disputes to the advantage of labor, whenever the Presidency deemed it politically advisable.

Act No. 14,250 constitutes the basic piece of legislation regulating collective agreements.[14] It establishes procedures and regulations concerning their legal status, governmental approval, publication, coverage, negotiation, expiration, etc. Article 14 provides for the appointment of a joint committee (*comisión paritaria*) to handle problems arising under the agreement. These committees are set up at the request of any of the parties to the agreement and consist of an equal number of employers' and employees' representatives presided over by an official appointed by the Ministry of Labor and Welfare. Grievances not settled by such joint committees and, in general, individual complaints of noncompliance with labor legislation are handled by the labor courts.[15]

During the last years of Perón's dictatorship, it became the practice to negotiate or revise collective agreements having a duration of two years. Most contracts throughout the nation were negotiated and expired at the same time. Of course, this practice had great repercussions on both the political and economic fields. About 500 collective agreements were in force when Perón fell, the majority of which should have expired in February 1956. On February 17, 1956, the Revolutionary government issued Legislative Decree No. 2,739,[16] extending the force of all collective agreements until their revision could be approved by the Ministry of Labor and Welfare. Furthermore, Article 8 of the decree required all new agreements to contain certain provisions regarding equal pay for work of equal value performed by male and female workers; the maintenance of general working conditions and workers' employment status, remuneration, and job classifications, contained in the expiring agreements, unless they were considered to interfere with the national goal of increasing productivity; and deletion of provisions in current agreements which were harmful to productivity (this could be done *ex officio* by a committee of ministers). As long as they did not violate the above-mentioned requirements, lengthen

[14] For a more detailed analysis of the Act, see Fillol, T.: *op. cit.*, pp. 104–106; or U. S. Department of Labor, *op. cit.*, pp. 15–16.
[15] For further information on labor courts in Argentina, see Antokoletz, D.: *Derecho del Trabajo y Previsión Social*, Vol. II, 2nd. Ed. (Buenos Aires, G. Kraft Ltda., 1953), pp. 189–206.
[16] República Argentina, Ministerio de Trabajo y Seguridad Social: *Convenios Colectivos de Trabajo* (Buenos Aires, Dirección Nacional de Estadística y Censos, 1958), pp. 87–90.

the workday, or impair the health of the workers, employers were authorized to adopt measures facilitating an increase in productivity. These measures could include displacements of manpower, *the institution of "moral and material incentives,"* and *special agreements with workers and employees to promote productivity.* Article 9 repealed all legal, conventional, and statutory provisions which prescribed joint unionization of the technical and supervisory staff with the working force. Article 10 ruled that all new collective agreements should have a minimum duration of eighteen months and gave the Ministry of Labor and Welfare power to prevent the joint expiration of all agreements. Article 13 made new agreements compulsory for all workers and employers within the activity covered by the agreements. Finally, Articles 11, 12, and 14 provided for compulsory arbitration of disagreements on the terms of contracts to be renewed in 1956 before an Arbitration Tribunal composed of three representatives of the Ministry of Labor and Welfare and two of the Ministry of Industry and Commerce. This tribunal was organized and constituted in July 1956.

Some bargaining committees began their talks early in April. Others did not organize until much later. Furthermore, in practically all cases serious disagreements unduly delayed the signing of new contracts. Obviously in order to accelerate this process, the Ministry of Labor and Welfare declared in August 1956 that Legislative Decree No. 2,739 actually limited the functions of bargaining committees to matters relating to wages and productivity.[17] Far from fulfilling its intended purpose, this obviously inaccurate interpretation, restricting to a great extent the autonomy of the bargaining parties, and contrary to the essence of free bargaining procedures, caused only greater enmity to arise between government and labor. The situation worsened in November, when the revolutionary government issued Decree No. 20,414 providing for the executive (rather than the Arbitration Tribunal) to settle disputes arising out of disagreement on the terms of new labor contracts in state enterprises.[18] In other words, this meant that the state was to be both judge and party to such disputes.

Between 1956 and 1957, 405 collective agreements were approved by the main office of the Ministry of Labor and Welfare (others were approved by regional delegations of the said ministry) under the regulations of Decree No. 2,739. Only 255 of these agreements were settled by the bargaining committees, as many as 150 (37 per cent) having had recourse to the Arbitration Tribunal. Twenty-one per cent of the 405 contracts were to expire in July 1957; 37 per cent, between August and December of the same year; 24 per cent, in January 1958; and the rest (18 per cent), in February

[17] Belaúnde: *op. cit.,* p. 14.
[18] *Ibid.,* p. 15.

or later.[19] However, in January 1957, the revolutionary government issued Legislative Decree No. 824, extending for one year, counted from their expiration date onwards, all collective agreements in force at that time. This resolution was part of a campaign against inflation and, to some extent, also attributable to delays in the formation of bargaining committees responsible for the renegotiation of labor agreements expiring in July. However valid these motives, the measure exemplified another case of government meddling in private contracts, which is neither legal nor desirable to improve already stumbling industrial relations.

Perhaps some reference should be made to the usual contents of collective agreements in order to give the reader a more precise idea of their evolution since 1943. As has been already mentioned, collective agreements normally incorporate or widen legally established minimum standards in wages, hours, conditions of work, and family allowances, while complementing them with provisions for a number of benefits not required by law. Although, according to the Argentine Commercial Code, "closed shop" clauses are illegal in Argentina, in practice many agreements also contain some form of union security clause, admitted in the past in case law, and providing some safeguards for unorganized workers.[20] In addition, collective agreements usually regulate working conditions, workers' classifications, wage scales, grievance procedures, and modes of wage payments. They sometimes also include provisions with regard to the establishment and financing of apprenticeship courses, contributions to several union funds, levy of union dues, and the like.

Although in 1946 his government announced that the *right to strike* "constitutes an incontrovertible principle of labor legislation and an element of inestimable value in the struggle for dignified living and working conditions," [21] in practice Perón, throughout his regime, greatly curtailed labor's right to strike, outlawing and ruthlessly repressing any strike he disapproved. The legal instruments which gave the dictatorship the power to outlaw almost any strike it wished ranged from the "Crimes against the Security of the State" law, which made "illegal" and thus subject to repression by the state all strikes affecting federal, provincial, or municipal public administrative offices and those private and semiofficial enterprises

---

[19] *Ibid.*, pp. 26–30.

[20] Vernengo, R.: *op. cit.*, p. 599; and Garzón Ferreyra, I.: *op. cit.*, p. 104.

[21] Quoted in Krotoschin, E.: *Curso de Legislación del Trabajo* (Buenos Aires, Editorial Depalma, 1950), p. 333. It is interesting to note that nowhere in Perón's 1949 Constitution, in the "Rights of the Worker," or in the elaboration of these rights in the text of the Constitution was labor's right to strike even mentioned. For an accurate analysis of Perón's labor policies up until 1950, see Alexander, R.: *The Peron Era* (New York, Columbia University Press, 1951).

performing services "in the public interest"; to Article 7 of Law No. 13,985 which severely punished "sabotage" activities which would endanger "the nation's military, economic, financial, social, scientific, or industrial development" — a catch-all provision which made almost any strike subject to repression.[22]

The 1955 Revolution modified these procedures. In December 1955 it repealed the above-mentioned laws but enacted in September 1957 the so-called "Right-to-Strike" law, providing for a practically obligatory system of governmental conciliation and arbitration of collective disputes in the federal capital (Buenos Aires), and determining when a strike was to be declared "illegal." [23] This law was in turn repealed in July 1958 by the newly elected Frondizi administration, which has since enacted (in August 1958) the Workingmen's Organizations Law,[24] which in Article 39 states that:

> For the purposes of defending their occupational interests, whether individual or collective, employees shall have the following essential rights:
>
> (a) to petition the authorities or their employers, either directly or through their representatives;
>
> (b) to elect their representatives in full freedom;
>
> (c) to take concerted action for the purpose of collective bargaining, mutual assistance or protection;
>
> (d) to bargain collectively through industrial associations with trade status;
>
> (e) to assemble, organize and become members of an industrial organization.

The 1958 Workingmen's Organizations Law also provides for a body, called the National Industrial Relations Council, with power to decide whether employers have been guilty of *unfair practices* contrary to the ethics of industrial relations. The council consists of seven members, of whom two represent the employers, two the employees, and three the government. It has jurisdiction throughout the country and makes decisions by simple majority vote. The law deems "unfair," practices such as subsidizing a workers' organization either directly or indirectly; impeding or hindering an employee from joining an industrial organization, or encouraging him by unfair means to join a particular union; making reprisals against an employee on account of his trade-union activities; and refusing to bargain collectively with employees in accordance with the legal procedure.

[22] See Unsain, A.: *Ordenamiento de las Leyes Obreras Argentinas,* 4th Edition (Buenos Aires, El Ateneo, 1952), p. 395; and Deveali, M.: *Curso de Derecho Sindical y de la Previsión Social* (Buenos Aires, Víctor P. de Zavalía, 1954), p. 305

[23] See also Fillol, T.: *op. cit.,* pp. 112–113; or U. S. Dept. of Labor, *op. cit.,* pp. 16–17.

[24] República Argentina, *Boletín Oficial* (September 24, 1958), No. 18747, p. 1; also I.L.O.: *Legislative Series, 1958 — Argentina 1* (Geneva, May–June, 1959).

In addition, the state has also encouraged or introduced some labor-management *co-operation schemes* designed to accomplish particular national goals — the National Productivity Institute, for example, set up in 1957 and designed to boost productivity in industry through the centralization and co-ordination of research and the dissemination of technical knowledge. In practice, however, statutory schemes such as this do not seem to have worked out as desired, mainly because of lack of interest and ineffective collaboration among the parties concerned.

Some Consequences

The acceleration of welfare legislation and decrees dictated by governments since the mid-1940's have had a powerful effect upon the cost structure of industry. Not only have money wages increased sharply (roughly 2,700 per cent between 1943 and 1958), but so have social charges. In 1958, the numerous contributions to social funds and direct payments to his employees for which national legislation and contractual arrangements make the typical industrial employer responsible amounted to approximately 70 per cent of his basic payroll.[25] Furthermore, labor legislation has often been administered in such a way as to make it extremely difficult for a company to discharge its employees. Since even closing down does not end a company's liability to its workers, new firms have often been deterred from opening up, and existing establishments have shown a consistent unwillingness to expand operations.

In many instances, benefit schemes accorded to the workers by government have placed an unexpected and undue burden upon employers. The most famous example is the issue of the *aguinaldo* (thirteenth-month pay) decree. Promulgated on December 20, 1945, at the height of the Presidential campaign for the February 1946 elections and obviously designed to win the labor vote for Perón, the decree required all commercial and industrial establishments to pay the annual bonus as of December 31.[26]

Furthermore, cases such as the above inevitably have inflationary consequences. This is important because the disturbing effects of inflation have been the direct cause of most industrial conflicts during the last decade. For instance, ever since Perón inaugurated such practices, governments have considered it advisable to "freeze" wages and prices in order to combat inflation. Trade unions have vigorously protested against such actions, causing the atmosphere of labor-management relations to deteriorate and strikes to increase as a result. In the face of industrial

---

[25] U. S. Dept. of Labor: *op. cit.,* pp. 18 and 22–23; and República Argentina, DiNIE, *op. cit.,* p. 61.

[26] See also Blanksten, G.: *Peron's Argentina* (Chicago, The University of Chicago Press, 1953), p. 263.

strife, the maintenance of order has made it necessary for government to intervene. Such intervention has occasionally resulted in the arbitrary regulation of strikes, and more often in the grant by decree of emergency wage increases. Frequent massive wage increases by themselves foster inflation. But the situation has usually been worsened by the provision that such increases should have "retroactive effect." Since such decrees are usually vaguely worded and leave room for different interpretations, no company is sure about the exact amount it will have to pay retroactively to its workers. Labor costs and social charges are thus at best uncertain for some time thereafter, and this means naturally a higher price rise than the increase in costs would warrant. In other words, "creeping" inflation is given additional stimulus. The inflationary process is further spurred by the fact that most companies must have recourse to bank loans to meet retroactive payments; interest rates rise, and so do costs and prices. Wage-increase decrees with retroactivity clauses have of course great propaganda value. Perón promulgated them periodically. Unfortunately, postdictatorship governments have not abandoned their use.

Finally, we must also point out that one of the greatest harms inflicted by Perón's dictatorship upon industry and business was the systematic attack on businessmen's and management's initiative and independence. Paradoxically enough, both labor and employers were forced to rely heavily on government during the dictatorship. For instance, for an industrial establishment to prosper, it was almost compulsory to take sides openly with the administration and collaborate actively in all "voluntary" contribution programs set up to finance Perón's political propaganda machinery.[27] This not only destroyed the initiative, the independence, and to a great extent the moral values of the business and industrial communities, but it also set a precedent of reliance on government which may be very difficult to uproot. But we should also note that in spite of dictatorial pressures, a habit of dependence on government would not have grown and taken strong roots unless a tendency towards dependence — here again, the characteristic "need dependency" of the Argentine — had been latent in the first place.

PERSONNEL ADMINISTRATION

We have already pointed out that the middle layers of the Argentine society do not constitute a uniform and coherent "social class." Thus, with respect to their views of the working elements, some middle-

[27] See, for instance, Johnson, J.: *Political Change in Latin America* (Stanford, California, Stanford University Press, 1958), pp. 118–119.

sector individuals have only a paternalistic interest in, and understanding of, labor; some have inherited an almost blind abhorrence for the labor movement; others know the working classes and understand them because they have only recently risen from among their ranks. The same can be said of the Argentine managerial force, almost all of whose members are "middle sector" men. Within the business world in general and the industrial-management community in particular, however, a pattern of relations with labor based on a common approach to the working elements typically emerges. Labor tends still to be considered as just another commodity whose services are to be bought as cheaply as possible. At best, the typical entrepreneur may take a paternalistic interest in his workers, but although he may give them greater recognition as individuals than other employers, he may be prompted to impose his will as a right and to expect unquestioning obedience.

Of course, *peronismo* and the enforcement of labor legislation brought about a drastic change in the external or verbalized behavior of employers with respect to labor. For instance, voluntary schemes to handle labor-management relations have acquired considerable importance in highly developed industries. In fact, ever since World War I, joint bodies of one kind or another were set up in some industries to iron out minor troubles, help settle disputes between individual workers and management, handle grievances, etc. But it is only in recent years that most collective agreements in the manufacturing and extractive industries provide for the appointment of shop stewards, periodical conferences between management and workers' representatives, formation of advisory committees of workers to deal with questions of internal personnel administration, and the like.[28]

Furthermore, since 1957, employers have been (at least theoretically) confronted with another problem: the question of workers' participation in management and in the profits made by the undertaking. As has been already mentioned, a constitutional amendment (1957) promises both to every employee. Of course, the amendment is too recent to have had yet widespread influence in industry or labor legislation. However, employers recognize that they may have to comply with such provisions in the future. But under practically no circumstances have private employers hitherto given the worker much say in the running of industrial establishments. The same is not wholly true of the government, which, for instance, granted the railworkers' unions participation in the management of state railways in February 1960. The practice of profit sharing, on the other hand, is fairly widespread. Dirección Nacional de Industrias

---

[28] Vernengo, R.: *op. cit.*, p. 614. See also Argimón, C.: *Relaciones del Trabajo y Colaboración en la Empresa* (Buenos Aires, G. Kraft Ltda., 1954).

del Estado, or DiNIE (in charge of a large number of state industrial enterprises), for example, has such plans, and so do many private establishments. From the point of view of management, however, these plans have encountered in practice a serious inconvenience: although there is no legislation specifically regulating profit-sharing schemes, the courts have usually determined that profit-sharing payments are part of a worker's total remuneration and thus an element to be taken into consideration in the calculation of pension contributions, severance payments, indemnities, compensations, and the like.[29]

In general, however, management emerged from the Perón experience steadfastly convinced that the average worker is lazy, dishonest, irresponsible, unreliable, antagonistic, gullible, an easy prey of the demagogue and the charlatan, and indifferent to progress and the common good beyond the personal satisfaction of his vices. The Argentine manager does not doubt that most of his own workers are skillful, alert, adaptable, and creative. But most managers believe that workers are unwilling or unable to apply such gifts to useful (industrial) purposes. Therefore, all blame for the nation's political, economic, and social troubles is put on labor and indirectly on government for fomenting the workers' natural faults and indolence. In industrial and business circles, there seems to be a lack of awareness that at least part of the responsibility for the retardation of Argentine industrial development is as much attributable to the employers' past and present mistakes as it is to labor and government.

An illustration of management's general approach with regard to labor questions is its attitude towards collective bargaining. Usually, neither employers nor unions go into collective-bargaining procedures having taken care to examine with due anticipation background data, what the fundamental issues are, what workers or employers presumably expect to achieve, or even what the other party will demand. The consequences of such an approach are fairly obvious. Ignorance is best dealt with by adopting a defensive and unconciliatory, thus safe but negative, position. Under such circumstances, it is not surprising that approximately 37 per cent of all collective agreements signed between 1956 and 1957 were settled by the Arbitration Tribunal, as has been mentioned earlier in this chapter.

It seems needless to point out that this attitude, as well as the general approach of Argentine employers towards the working force, can be accounted for in terms of the basic personality of the Argentine (and

[29] Perez Paton, R.: "La Participación del Trabajo en las Ganancias del Capital," in Librería "El Ateneo" (ed.): *Estudios de Derecho del Trabajo en Memoria de Alejandro M. Unsain* (Buenos Aires, 1954), p. 396.

especially of his orientation with regard to basic human nature and the valued personality type), and also in terms of the high need dependency and strong need aggression conspicuous in the Argentine society. Because he possesses the latter cultural traits, an individual feels secure and psychologically satisfied when participating in interpersonal situations where the relationship of authority has been unequivocally defined. When he faces someone else with the authority relationship unsettled, he often adopts a defensive position and seeks to handle the situation the only way he has learned to — in terms of power.

Summarizing, Argentine industrial managers (and businessmen in general) seem to be sitting in a glass cage, watching the day-to-day deterioration of industrial relations, blaming labor and government for Argentina's economic retardation, but at the same time discharging their burden of responsibility for solving the industrial problem on the already overloaded shoulders of the state. They know that, in the past, government has been conspicuously unable to manage the nation's industrialization process. But they still insist that the state should not only provide the necessary protectionist climate to foster industrialization, but also (perhaps by magic!) provide industry with a docile, obedient, disciplined, productive labor force. Industrialists in general do not seem to have given any thought to the fact that the productivity, motivation, and cooperation of labor are primarily determined by the management which employs it and not by the more or less enlightened social and economic policies of government.

The above comments apply, of course, to today's average manager and especially to the "old guard" within the managerial ranks. There is reason to believe that the new crop of managers which will start replacing the senior cadres during the 1960's may not abide by the same rules and cling to the same philosophies as their predecessors. They have been brought up in a rapidly changing, troubled world; in college they have been (perhaps too much) exposed to leftist ideals and theories of social justice; twelve years of tyranny have undoubtedly lighted in them the flame of justice and democracy; and, above all, they are fervent nationalists sincerely desiring Argentina's economic and social progress. If time, responsibilities, and the adequate inculcation of the principles and methods of modern management (especially as they apply to industrial relations) can temper their youthful impulses without extinguishing the flame of their ideals, Argentina's future may be indeed bright.

But is the society as a whole — and labor particularly — ready to accept new principles, ideas, and concepts of social and industrial organization? The next chapter, dealing with Argentine labor, will help in partially answering this question.

5 ARGENTINE LABOR

THE agricultural-pastoral character of the Argentine economy; the traditional *patrón-peón* relationship in which farm workers generally saw all their food and shelter needs well cared for by landowners who usually exhibited a suitable, "paternalistic" sense of responsibility for the well-being of their workers; the continuous inflow of ambitious immigrants willing to undertake any available job in order to realize their dream of riches; and, in general, the passive value orientations typical of the national character, coupled with the Argentine's characteristic drive towards aggression and dependency on superiors, deprived the Argentine labor movement of a steady evolution in which the pride of workmanship and a tradition of responsibility towards the community could have been cultivated. Instead, the history of Argentine trade unions is largely an account of internal strife, of disunity, struggle, and rancor.

An Argentine labor authority has written that over certain periods in the past, workers' hatred of each other has been far greater than their animosity towards employers; and that in many instances a trade union has been nothing but a committee and a rubber stamp on a sheet of paper.[1] All major currents of political and economic thought of the last one hundred years have been represented at some point or other of the Argentine labor movement. More importantly, although there have been notable exceptions, Argentine unions have generally placed great emphasis on rights and immediate gains rather than on permanent constructive achievements. The labor movement has often shown an unfortunate lack of awareness of its duties and responsibilities towards the public and employers. Many Argentine intellectuals, influenced by Marx, have been prone to interpret this characteristic of the labor movement as a product of the workers' class rancor. This of course is mostly a myth, as we shall see.

[1] Unsain, A. M., in *Legislación del Trabajo,* Vol. II (Buenos Aires, Ed. Abeledo, 1926), p. 322. For a detailed analysis of the history of Argentine trade-unionism, see Fillol, T.: *Industrial Relations in the Economic Development of Argentina,* unpublished S.M. thesis (Massachusetts Institute of Technology, 1960), pp. 50–74. Further bibliographical information on Argentine labor is listed at the end of this book.

Cultural Barriers to Unionism

Describing the Argentine social situation at the turn of the century, José M. Ramos Mejía, an eminent Argentine sociologist of that period, pointed out that great European-like mass upheavals did not develop and could have not developed in Argentina because the lower classes were not united (as in Europe) by miserable living conditions or class hatred.[2] This continued to be true throughout the first half of the century. Farm workers have customarily enjoyed an adequate degree of security — at least they have not suffered more in periods of deep decline in world markets than they have benefited from export prosperity in other years. The impact of unemployment either in farming or in nonagricultural activities has never been really serious, although partial underemployment, with its negative effect on real incomes, has occasionally been fairly widespread.[3] The Argentine diet (as measured by the calorie supply per capita) was the world's most adequate in early postwar years,[4] while Argentine living standards and consumption levels have been Latin America's highest throughout this half-century. Under such circumstances, it is hard to believe that the Argentine masses were profoundly dissatisfied with their standards of living, as Perón insisted. What they were looking for were targets on which to vent their anxiety, rage, and need aggression. Although to a great extent imaginary (with the exception of housing shortages experienced by part of the rural-urban migrant population), unsatisfactory living standards appealed to the masses as a plausible target. In other words, they were induced by their leader to *think* and *feel* — and, in response to their high need dependency, they willingly accepted their leader's indication — that they were dissatisfied with their living standards, while relieving their rage and need aggression through the clamorous expression of such discontent. Unconsciously,

[2] Ramos Mejía, J. M.: *Las Multitudes Argentinas* (Buenos Aires, Guillermo Kraft Ltda., 1952), p. 344.

[3] See Hanson, S.: *Economic Development in Latin America* (Washington, D. C., The Inter-American Affairs Press, 1951), p. 66; and Ortiz, R.: *Historia Económica de la Argentina*, pp. 185–6 and 193–7. The maximum number of unemployed workers during the Great Depression hardly reached 260,000, or roughly 5 per cent of the total economically active population (5,018,000 in 1933).

[4] Food supplies bought by Argentine consumers in 1945–1946 provided an average of 3,190 calories per head per day compared with 3,130 in the United States and 3,060 in Canada. The same figures, however, for 1954–1955 show 2,840 calories per head per day in Argentina, 3,070 in the United States, and 3,030 in Canada. Thus, while the calorie supply per capita per day was 22.7 per cent higher than requirements in 1945–1946 — the world's highest figure for the early postwar period — it was only 9.2 per cent higher than requirements in 1954–1955 (in Argentina, of course). The consumption of manufactured goods, such as textiles, is much lower in Argentina than in the United States because of their high prices relative to wages. Source: United Nations, *Report on the World Social Situation* (New York, 1957), p. 61.

however, they could not have felt class rancor or the bitterness which arises through years of *material* deprivation; otherwise, it would be impossible to explain their behavior on August 31, 1955, when they refused to follow Perón's tacit but clear order to destroy the "oligarchy" by plundering Buenos Aires' aristocratic quarters.

Actually, throughout Argentina's political history, the landowning élite — or more properly the Conservatives — were far from being the labor-oppressing ogres Perón used to portray in his propaganda tirades. Certainly, labor legislation before 1943 would scarcely have been enacted had it not been for the vigor and courage of a group of Socialist party legislators who fought for the workers in Congress. But Socialists were only a small minority in Congress (sometimes less than half a dozen; in 1932, when the Radicals were not allowed to run candidates, they were forty-four).[5] Although the direct or indirect representatives of landed interests, on the other hand, steadily enjoyed a wide majority, they permitted a fair amount of social legislation to be enacted. In fact, up to 1942 Argentine labor legislation stood among the most advanced in Latin America, only surpassed by that of Mexico and of Uruguay, while Chilean labor legislation stood at approximately the same level as the Argentine.[6] This suggests that notwithstanding Perón's claim that *his* administration brought social justice to Argentina (a claim which seems to have convinced many people in Argentina and foreign countries), much had been achieved in the field of social legislation during the supposedly labor-hating, pre-1943 administrations. No doubt, the social reforms completed under Perón's direction were numerous; some of them were very necessary; and they did correct many injustices. But it would be a fundamental mistake to believe (as some authors do) that labor legislation and social welfare were first introduced to Argentina by Perón. Similarly, it would be erroneous to assert that prior to 1943, the aristocracy as a whole was *anti*-labor. In fact, *it could not have cared less.* It was absolutely indifferent to labor's needs and wishes. So far as the Conservative party was concerned, the labor movement was little more than obnoxious. On *this* account, as was mentioned in Chapter 3, the aristocracy should certainly be indicted. As in other aspects of the national life, it refused to see the reality, to listen to half the country — in short, it *ignored* the country and the labor movement with it.

These considerations lead to the following conclusion. If Argentine workers had possessed the necessary *esprit de corps* to build a strong union movement; if they had had the will to *unite* and *co-operate* in the

[5] Alexander, R.: *The Peron Era* (New York, Columbia University Press, 1951), p. 11.
[6] Tieffenberg, D.: *La Legislación Obrera en el Régimen Peronista* (Buenos Aires, Ediciones Populares Argentinas, 1956), pp. 39 ff.

disorderly fight they conducted for their rights and progress; if they had been psychologically capable of building, by their own initiative, a strong organization dedicated to their common benefit; if they had been able to generate from within their ranks, not a weak leadership torn by factionalism and theoretical debate, but creative, progressive-minded leadership ready and able to initiate constructive solutions, then unions would have found little resistance on the part of government in their search for the advancement of the working classes. At first sight, this statement may appear erroneous. It seems obvious that since the aristocracy was naturally eager to maintain the *status quo* and its members were, directly or indirectly, the government, they would have sternly repelled any attempt to disrupt the established social order. The clue lies in the meaning of the term *status quo*. For the big landowner, it meant neither industry nor industrial (urban) labor, since he consciously or unconsciously looked down upon or was completely uninterested in either one of them. By *status quo* the aristocracy, consciously or unconsciously, meant the *estancia,* Buenos Aires' exclusive clubs, and assured revenue from the sale of agricultural or livestock products to Europe. None of these would have been threatened, at least in the short run (and there is enough historical and cultural evidence that the Argentine does not look beyond such a point), by industrialization and trade-unionism, especially because the organization of farm workers is practically impossible to achieve in the immense pampas, as it was proved during the Perón regime.

It is obvious, however, that social reforms could have been accomplished only through the pressure of interested groups themselves. The formation of strong workers' organizations would have greatly enhanced the probabilities of achieving such reforms by orderly, nonrevolutionary means. But real, militant, independent trade-unionism was — and still is — practically impossible to accomplish in Argentina. The Argentine national character has not only been inimical to the development of a progressive-minded aristocracy capable of thinking beyond its own circle and benefit but, as has been already mentioned, it has also not permitted the emergence of a "community spirit" within the society — a "co-operative-mindedness" among Argentine people which would have enhanced the chances of worker collaboration and unity at the industrial-organization level. Specifically, the cultural incapacity of the Argentine worker to initiate trade-unionism can be best explained in terms of his Being-orientation or, alternatively, in terms of one of the most common manifestations of this basic value orientation, *personalismo.* This cultural characteristic means that there is in every phase of life a basic distrust in the large and impersonal organization — a corporation or a union, for instance—because such an entity is regarded as being over and above the individuals who are part of it. Most of the economic life is thus based on the personal relation between superior and subordinate. Similarly, in matters of social organization, it is the personal relationship between individuals that is important. One cannot talk to, argue with, or deal personally with banks, governments, companies, or unions, "They in themselves have no life, no vitality, no souls. Only people are possessed of such characteristics, and these are the things in life that count." [7]

If *personalismo* is fundamental to an understanding of the Argentine worker's basic mistrust of, and thus his inability to initiate, unionism, it is also fundamental to an explanation of his political behavior, especially the apparent contradiction presented by the fact that, while unable to trust or co-operate with large organizations, Argentine workers were the pillars of the largest mass movement—*peronismo*—the country has ever witnessed.

INDUSTRIALIZATION, URBANIZATION, AND "PERONISM"

In political life, *personalismo* expresses itself as "the exaltation of, and identification with, the leader—el 'caudillo'—at the expense of principles or party platforms." [8] It is obvious that this is simultaneously the best definition of "Peronism"—loyalty to the man, Perón, rather than formulation *by* the working masses of their own political and economic goals. To some extent, the same definition applies to the masses' idolization of Irigoyen a generation earlier. The scope and consequences, however, of "Irigoyenism" and "Peronism" bear no comparison with each other, as has been mentioned earlier. Apart from the obvious differences between the methods, ambitions, and honesty of the two leaders, Perón came to power at an extremely propitious time; he found the country in the midst of a process of social transformation which made the masses far "readier" to receive him and his demagoguery than they had been in Irigoyen's time.

During the period 1937–1947, the number of workers employed in secondary industries increased annually by an average of 42,000, while the number of persons entering the total labor force each year averaged only about 40,000. Furthermore, tertiary industries showed during the

[7] Whyte, W., and Holmberg, A.: *Human Problems of U. S. Enterprise in Latin America, 1956* (Ithaca, N. Y., New York State School of Industrial and Labor Relations, Cornell University), p. 3.

[8] *Ibid.*, p. 3. We must also keep in mind that "need dependency" is another essential element of *personalismo*. Argentines satisfied their high dependency drives by finding a leader who would make all decisions for them.

same period a pronounced increase in employment: between 1940–44 and 1945–49, for instance, employment indices rose from 125.8 to 142.9 in commerce, and from 167.4 to 250.7 for state employees (1925–29 = 100). Also taking into account the fact that immigration stopped for all practical purposes after 1930 (it did not resume until 1947), this means that during the period under consideration secondary industries by themselves absorbed more than the total number of persons entering the labor force, while the total demand for labor exceeded by at least 80 or 100 per cent the supply determined by normal demographic growth in the absence of any immigration.[9] This process had two obvious consequences: first, full employment; and second, the mass emigration of rural workers to the cities.

In September 1940, a Department of Labor study indicated that there were 180,700 unemployed workers in the Republic, more than half of them in the city of Buenos Aires: 60,000 in industry and commerce, 21,000 in transportation and communications, 15,000 in the building-construction and metal trades, etc.[10] Percentagewise, these figures were still high, since the maximum number of unemployed workers registered during the depression hardly reached 260,000 (in 1932). Full employment had already been reached, however, by the end of 1942, at least six months before the 1943 military revolution and ten months before an obscure Army colonel, Juan Perón, was made director of the national Department of Labor. It was maintained through 1947–48, when immigration resumed.

Full employment, besides affording opportunities for vertical and horizontal social mobility, directly contributes to improving workers' living standards. Most importantly, however, it greatly strengthens the workers' bargaining power. Conceivably, given this basic position of strength, workers could have gained, if properly organized, and without government help, the same or even greater benefits than they actually received under Perón's "protection." In 1943, however, the government took over the direction of the labor movement. As a result, workers regarded the benefits they received as coming from the state, a homage it did not fully deserve.

Until around 1930, the increases in population — over and above normal demographic growth — of the larger Argentine cities were mainly the consequence of European immigration. Between that period and 1947, how-

[9] Germani, G.: "Algunas Repercusiones Sociales de los Cambios Económicos en la Argentina," summarized in *Ciencias Sociales,* Pan American Union, Vol. III, No. 18 (Dec. 1952), p. 152; and United Nations, C.E.P.A.L.: *El Desarrollo Económico de la Argentina,* Part I (Mexico, 1959), p. 40
[10] Pan American Union: *Labor Trends and Social Welfare in Latin America, 1941 and 1942* (Washington, D. C., July 1943), p. 6.

ever, European immigration was replaced as a source of city growth by the massive influx of internal migrants. Between 1943 and 1947, about 900,000 to 1,000,000 persons, or 20 per cent of the rural population in 1943, are believed to have moved into urban areas. During the same period, Greater Buenos Aires (including the capital and seven centers within the urban agglomeration) gained approximately 750,000 inhabitants, nearly 600,000 of them internal migrants, and by 1947 it contained 29 per cent of the national population.[11]

Two main consequences can be attributed to this exodus to the cities. First, the largest cities, and particularly Buenos Aires, experienced acute housing shortages. The situation was worsened by rent controls instituted by the revolutionary government in 1943 as a means of redistributing national income in favor of urban areas. This measure, of course, completely discouraged new private construction for rental. Therefore, high percentages of migrant workers were forced into peripheral shantytowns, locally called *villas miseria*. Adequate housing was not available despite relatively high incomes. The extent of this problem was only made public after the fall of Perón by the National Housing Commission.[12] It revealed that although government-assisted construction of dwellings *for sale* had been belatedly undertaken, black-market practices (not always unofficial) had become common in housing transfers, and that it had been almost impossible for low-income migrant families without savings to find new dwellings. According to the same report, the *villas miseria* of Greater Buenos Aires still housed about 100,000 persons (2 per cent of the city's population) in 1956. Several of these shantytowns had risen on land otherwise unused because it was subject to flooding or near garbage dumps.

Second, urbanization greatly contributed to the formation of an amorphous human mass in and around the large cities (and especially Buenos Aires) which built the basis for the greatest socio-political mass movement the country had yet undergone. Undoubtedly, the amount of social adjustment necessary through an industrialization and urbanization process is far smaller in Argentina than elsewhere in Latin America. The lack of any sharp ethnic or cultural contrasts between rural and urban Argentines, together with the fact that the nation's labor supply, either directly or indirectly, is derived to a great extent from southern Europe, has made Argentine labor more adaptable to the requirements of industrialization than working forces of other Latin American countries with large percentages of Indian population and well-entrenched native traditions and

[11] Germani, G.: *op. cit.,* as cited in United Nations, *Report on the World Social Situation* (New York, 1957), p. 175.
[12] República Argentina, Comisión Nacional de la Vivienda: *Plan de Emergencia. Informe Elevado al Poder Ejecutivo Nacional* (Buenos Aires, April 1956).

ways of life. Furthermore, official Argentine publications suggest that a high percentage of the population that migrates to the big cities comes from populated centers with more than 2,000 inhabitants and from the small cities (generally from the suburbs and outskirts), which means that they adapt themselves very soon to the environment of the large cities.[13]

This does not mean, however, that the process of industrialization and urbanization during the period under consideration was exempt from social consequences. Actually, less than 200,000 workers out of 1,000,000 migrants were absorbed by industry between 1943 and 1947. A great percentage of the rest had to find work as porters, hawkers and petty traders, construction workers, domestic servants, and the like — all low-paid activities plagued by underemployment or irregular employment. In any case, and whatever type of work they found in the large city, internal migration to industrial centers entailed a change to a different socio-economic environment. Therefore, besides their lack of training and technical skills, workers very often had to change their former occupation; and more often than not they were also forced to adhere to principles of regularity and punctuality at work and in general to the more rationalized and orderly ways of life of a large industrial city.[14]

To these factors we should also add the usual psychological readjustments accompanying any acculturation process. The loss of traditional forms of security makes migrant workers eager to find new reference groups with which to identify. Their self-image and sense of identity will be the more undermined if they are forced by seemingly uncontrollable circumstances into conditions of underemployment and unhealthful living quarters, as was the case in Buenos Aires. The result is the formation of a rootless human mass eager to follow any leader capable of supplying them with a new and attractive set of values and ideals. For such people, Perón's demagoguery had an almost compulsive appeal: not only did it satisfy their high need dependency, but it also furnished the migrant masses with a seemingly new and obviously attractive social and political philosophy; with a new, perfectly compatible reference group (the peronist unions); and with the necessary scapegoats (*yanquis* and *oligarcas,* among others) to make them rally behind a common banner and against whom they could vent their rage and thus satisfy their need aggression. It should be noted here that our statement

[13] Communication from the Ministry of Labor and Welfare, 1956, as cited in United Nations: *Report on the World Social Situation*, p. 175. In order to make the statement compatible with rural-urban employment statistics, it must be assumed that migrants from smaller towns are consequently replaced by migrants from rural areas.

[14] See also Germani: *op. cit.*, p. 154.

that peronist unions were readily accepted as a new "reference group" does not violate our assertion that Argentine workers, being "personalists," have a basic distrust in any kind of organization. Each individual, whether or not he is a "personalist," needs to see his behavior, which gives him a satisfying identity, validated by the acceptance of it by a "reference group," *his* reference group. In the absence of recognized acceptance, the individual would become socially alienated and thus susceptible to influence and change.[15]

Furthermore, the mass movement of population from rural areas to the cities, and the spread of mass media among them, greatly contributed to the creation of a new spirit of angered nationalism which swept the country during the mid-1940's. This emergence of *modern* nationalism, which has been defined as "the collective demand of frustrated people for direct action by the State,"[16] was partly due to the migrant's emotional need to replace the broken sense of local or provincial identification with new symbols of group membership at a higher, national level. This new type of nationalism gave Perón the opportunity to associate the old ruling élite with foreign exploitation and the agricultural economy, while presenting himself as the promoter of native values and a modern diversified economy.

Of course, these commentaries should not be interpreted as a suggestion that Perón's popularity was restricted to the migrant masses. We are only suggesting that these masses constituted the necessary basis and support on which Perón was able to build his unquestionably great and widespread popularity. The rest of the *peronista* electorate succumbed by conviction, apathy, interest, propaganda, frustration, or outright coercion. In 1947, for instance, a delegation of the American Federation of Labor visiting Argentina found that "it is not certain whether the apparent popularity of . . . Perón is due to the satisfaction of the working masses or . . . to the various techniques of psychological intimidation or coercion to which Mr. Perón has resorted."[17] Actually, the emergence of the *peronista* labor masses was the joint product of *both* the factors mentioned in the A.F. of L. report.

[15] See also Schein, E.: *Interpersonal Communication, Group Solidarity, and Social Influence* (Massachusetts Institute of Technology; unpublished address delivered to the International Council for Women Psychologists on August 28, 1958, in Washington, D. C.).

[16] Johnson, J. J.: *Political Change in Latin America* (Stanford, California, Stanford University Press, 1958), p. 188. See also Kahl, J. A.: "Some Social Concomitants of Industrialization and Urbanization," in *Human Organization*, Vol. 18, No. 2, p. 56. It should be noted that we do by no means imply that nationalism did not exist in Argentina before the 1940's. Here we specifically refer to the *spread* of a *new* type of nationalism as defined by Johnson.

[17] As quoted in Blanksten, G.: *Peron's Argentina* (Chicago, Ill., The University of Chicago Press, 1953), p. 326.

The main elements determining the unquestionable satisfaction of the working masses with Perón's social and economic policies are patent. The first factor is purely monetary. The average industrial worker made five times as much money in 1950 as in 1943. Of course, it did not follow that he was able to buy five times as much with this income. But wage levels of industrial (urban) workers increased more than consumer price levels from 1943 to 1948, and although their real incomes began to fall in 1949, workers did experience an increase of about 50 per cent in purchasing power between 1937 and 1948.[18] Second, and more important, Perón gave the worker *recognition,* the *feeling of being valued,* and the conviction that the government was genuinely interested in his needs and wishes. We will of course not discuss here how well- or ill-founded these feelings were. It is important, however, to realize that during the dictatorship, the Argentine worker saw for the first time his drive for recognition, accentuated by his basic Being-orientation, at least partially fulfilled. He felt important, someone to be catered to, someone whose wishes the government apparently respected. Not only was the worker given an extra month's pay but he also received the ostentatious protection of all sorts of laws. Every corner newsstand sold the text of these laws; the worker who carried one in his pocket felt for the first time in his life that he held a whip hand over his employer.[19] This situation had pernicious consequences for the economic life of the nation. And the reasons for it must again be found in the value-orientation profile of the society.

The Argentine worker was driven by his cultural traits to solve the new problem, in which the authority relationship had not yet been defined, in terms of power; to take advantage of the new situation to maximize his short-run benefit without giving any consideration to the effect his actions would have on the community at large and over the long pull; and to try to assert — obviously by aggressive means — his newly acquired status against those who questioned the legitimacy of it. This latter point should be particularly stressed. We must not forget that it was the *government* that claimed to recognize labor's status, rights, and privileges — *not the employer.* In other words, recognition and the feeling of being valued came from a force alien to the worker's prime source of (low) status in the society — his occupation. Moreover, this force was only indirectly responsible for his job, the axle on which his life and that of his family turned. It is therefore only natural that the worker should have sought to pin increased responsibilities for his job on the new and unexpected source of social recognition. On the other hand,

---

[18] *International Labor Review,* Statistical Supplement, Vol. LXXIII, 1956, pp. 62, 67, 82.
[19] Hanson, S.: *op. cit.,* p. 507.

at least unconsciously, the worker must have realized *himself* that his new position in society was illegitimate and artificial, since it was questioned by those who, in his eyes, bore prestige in society and particularly in the industrial environment. This feeling was a main source of internal conflict and anxiety which, by definition, would not have appeared had the worker been granted recognition *at work* rather than only by a force alien to it. As it happened, encouraged by their leader, workers not only sought increased protection from the government but overtly turned against the main barrier to general social recognition. Thus, employers were converted into one of the popularly sanctioned targets against which the working masses discharged their (cultural) rage and anxiety. This had, of course, direct effect on every phase of Argentina's economic life and particularly on industrial relations and the productivity of the labor force.

PRODUCTIVITY OF THE LABOR FORCE

Argentina is one of the very few countries in the world where, despite technological improvements, productivity per man was lower in 1955 than it was in 1945. During that period, the steady rise in the productivity of manufacturing industries was more than neutralized by a sharp decline in the productivity of practically all other sectors of the economy.[20] This was mainly the consequence of a defective distribution of manpower among the various types of employment. The proportion of the economically active population engaged in agricultural and livestock production decreased sharply despite inadequate progress in the production techniques of that sector of the economy. Furthermore, this process was not accompanied by a corresponding and necessary transfer of migrant population and, in general, of the increment in the total active population, to manufacturing industries. Instead, an exceptionally high proportion of it was diverted to construction, transportation, and service industries (commerce, banking, personal and domestic services, government, and the like).

As is shown in Table II, the ratio of the population engaged in manufacturing industries to the total economically active population *decreased* between 1940–1944 and 1955, a drastic reversal of the trend observed in previous decades. This occurred, of course, during a period in which

---

[20] See United Nations, C.E.P.A.L.: *El Desarrollo...*, pp. 36–41. *Productivity* is measured as physical output per man-year. In manufacturing industries, it increased at an average rate of 2.2 per cent annually between 1940–1944 and 1955. Construction and rail transportation were foremost among the sectors which showed sharp declines in productivity: 17.3 per cent in the former and 30 per cent in the latter between 1940–1944 and 1955.

TABLE II

Distribution of Population by Types of Employment (1900–1955)

Periods	Total Population	Economically Active Population	Directly Productive Sectors of the Economy						Non-Directly Productive Sectors of the Economy[a]
			Agriculture and Stock-raising	Manufacturing Industries	Mining and Construction	Transportation	Public Utilities	Total	
(a) POPULATION (IN THOUSANDS)									
1900–04	4,797	1,966 (41.6%)	738	396	94	92	15	1,380	616
1925–29	10,970	4,288 (39.1%)	1,539	890	212	218	52	2,911	1,377
1940–44	14,643	5,517 (37.7%)	1,838	1,310	215	248	85	3,969	1,821
1955	19,111	7,348 (38.4%)	1,916	1,655	415	434	142	4,562	2,786
(b) PER CENT OF ECONOMICALLY ACTIVE POPULATION									
1900–04		100	39.2	19.8	4.7	4.6	0.8	69.1	30.9
1925–29		100	35.9	20.8	4.9	5.1	1.2	67.9	32.1
1940–44		100	33.3	23.7	3.9	4.5	1.5	67.0	33.0
1955		100	26.1	22.5	5.6	5.9	1.9	62.1	37.9

[a] Includes state employees, employees of commercial and financial enterprises, and domestic and personal service workers.

SOURCE: United Nations, C.E.P.A.L.: *El Desarrollo Económico de la Argentina*, Part I (Mexico, 1959), p. 37.

industrialization was supposed to be the primary national objective. This phenomenon contributed by itself to the rise in productivity in manufacturing industries. But there are also related factors which are worth analyzing in greater detail.

Every Argentine employer is aware of the fact that skilled workers and technicians are still in seriously short supply. Argentine workers still insist on strict adherence to job classifications; they refuse to do work for which they are not specifically hired; they staunchly adhere to contract provisions limiting the number of machines to be operated by a worker; absenteeism (10 per cent), labor turnover, work stoppages, and go-slow movements plague industry; and large numbers of workers have more than one job, with consequent impairment of efficiency in each job.[21] Furthermore, at least up until 1956, when the revolutionary government abolished such practices, membership of supervisors in production workers' unions made the former unable to fulfill their functions adequately. Despite factors such as these, however, productivity has risen in manufacturing industries through the last two decades. This has a threefold explanation.

First, it partly reflects the private entrepreneur's unwillingness to employ more workers than barely necessary, on three main grounds: high direct and indirect labor costs; excessive dismissal payments as provided by legislation and collective agreements; and high occurrence of labor-management conflicts. Needless to say that up to 1955, none of these considerations carried much weight in determining the employment practices of the state. Second, the rate of capital accumulation and mechanization in manufacturing industries has been, if not adequate, at least positive — in contrast with that of the other sectors of the economy (especially transportation and public utilities), where the age and poor condition of machinery and equipment is patent. Finally, the rise in productivity must be also ascribed to the unquestionable adaptability of the Argentine labor force to new industrial jobs.

As we have seen in Chapter 4, the post-Perón revolutionary government issued in 1956 Legislative Decree No. 2,739, approving in principle the adoption of "moral and material incentives" which do not lengthen the workday or impair the health of the workers. The objective was to increase the productivity of the Argentine labor force. At the time the decree was issued, unions violently attacked the idea as antisocial, as disruptive of the workers' unity, and as bearing the seeds of chaos in the factory. Of course, much of the protest movement was simply part of the Peronist and Communist unions' policy of opposing any decision made

[21] U. S. Dept. of Labor: *Foreign Labor Information — Labor in Argentina* (Washington, D. C., Bureau of Labor Statistics, June 1959), p. 17.

by the military government that replaced Perón. But although most workers were undoubtedly eager to obtain the highest possible remuneration because of deterioration of their purchasing power, many workers showed "certain psychological resistance to the establishment of production incentives." [22] This resistance was no doubt reinforced by their being accustomed to obtaining higher remuneration by means of massive, government-decreed wage and salary increases.

Unfortunately, we do not have statistics that would give us an idea of how well incentive schemes have fared in private industry. On the other hand, Dirección Nacional de Industrias del Estado, or DiNIE, has published a very comprehensive and detailed account of the results obtained by production-incentive plans during 1956–1957 in state industrial enterprises.[23] (A large number of state industrial enterprises are administered by DiNIE.)

In principle, DiNIE sought to institute individual incentives wherever possible. In some cases, however, the affected workers and employees obtained through union pressure the establishment of collective incentives. Both direct and indirect workers participated in the plans. In some cases, participation was extended to supervisory and administrative personnel. The standards used to measure production increases vary from plan to plan but are in all cases similar to those usually applied in United States enterprises. Special bonuses were foreseen for those workers showing, at the end of the month, perfect or nearly perfect work attendance and punctuality. In all cases shown by the DiNIE report, the results were startling. For the specific months shown, production increases average between 30 and 40 per cent, reaching 250 per cent in particular cases. No significant differences are noticeable in the results obtained by collective as against individual incentive plans, but the published sample is too small to be conclusive on this point.

A general measure of the total effectiveness of these plans is given by figures comparing the increase in *hourly productivity* achieved during the fiscal year 1956–1957 by DiNIE enterprises and the *total* of the nation's manufacturing industry (including DiNIE). Although not all of DiNIE's enterprises established incentive schemes and the date of institution of the plans varied from case to case, DiNIE achieved a 3.5 per cent increase in hourly productivity during 1956–1957 compared with 0.4 per cent for the total of manufacturing industries.

Finally, a brief reference should be made to another problem bearing on the productivity of the labor force. Between 1943 and 1955, unskilled

---

[22] República Argentina, Dirección Nacional de Industrias del Estado (DiNIE): *Reseña de las Actividades del Organismo* (Buenos Aires, 1958), p. 64.
[23] *Ibid.*, pp. 63–83.

workers fared much better than skilled workers in the race between wage increases and inflation. Obviously, the smaller the wage difference paid for skilled and unskilled work, the less anxious an unskilled worker will be to acquire new technical abilities and thus to raise his productivity. The acute shortage of skilled labor and technicians in Argentina is a measure of the extent of this problem, which is particularly serious in a society which does not confer status on grounds of the expertness in *manual work* its members may possess.

POLITICAL UNIONISM

It has been suggested that since European practices and influences have often been instrumental in the development of Latin American labor movements, the political tendencies of early European and Latin American unions are the product of basically the same factors. According to the argument, legislation rather than collective bargaining has been the channel through which the European and Latin American labor movements have fought first their political battles for recognition and then their economic battles for an improvement of working conditions and living standards.[24] This is no doubt true as it applies to early, pre-Perón trade-unionism. Indeed, all through the beginnings of the Argentine labor movement the influence of European ideologies was patent.

On the other hand, to try to explain the political character of Argentine unionism under the dictatorship in such terms would be a fundamental mistake. Workers in some European countries, building generally united and coherent labor movements, were forced to gain recognition as equal partners, before they could effectively state their grievances and press for an improvement of their wages, hours, and working conditions in the economic arena. Thus, a strong, coherent, but *political* labor movement became initially the mouthpiece for the economic demands of European workers. In Argentina, on the other hand, a strong, coherent movement *could not have been achieved* without political leadership. Without the appearance, outside of the ranks of labor, of a national *political* leader whose decision it was to build powerful trade-unions, these unions would have never been formed in Argentina. And, we repeat, this was so not because of fear of repression but because of the cultural traits of the Argentine worker. Democratic labor unions, arguing out their policies within themselves, could not have grown because, by definition, workers with passive value orientations, high need dependency,

[24] See Steinbach, A., discussion of papers on "Labor Movements and Organizations," in *Labor, Management, and Economic Growth* (Ithaca, N. Y., Institute of International Industrial and Labor Relations, Cornell University, 1954), pp. 161–167.

and strong need aggression cannot co-operate in solving a complex problem *with equals*. A strong trade-union movement could have been formed only by someone appearing as *leader* and being followed by the working elements. And since local leaders themselves would have to be both autocratic and dependent, a *national autocratic leader* was bound to arise (and will again, unless some other focus for need dependency is created). In effect, it was such a leader (Perón) who gave the Argentine labor movement a strong political character, not the workers themselves, who chose the road of political trade-unionism.

The price to labor for this benevolent interest displayed by government was political backing of "Peronism," while the state regulated the activities of unions to such an extent that ordinarily the government in an independent capacity determined which labor laws would be enacted; which would be honored; and which and for whom standards, wages, and working conditions would apply at any point in time. Unions were thus encouraged and accustomed to place far greater emphasis upon political activities than on a collective-bargaining effort as it is generally understood in the United States. Unfortunately, after Perón's fall, political parties continued to foment such practices.

Since 1955, some unions have undoubtedly become increasingly mature, more capable of paying the costs of their trade-union activities. But although some unions seem to be perfectly aware of their past errors, labor's general approach to industrial relations and union matters seems to have changed little. The reasons are many. It is a characteristic of "personalism" that "once an idol has been erected, it is very rarely taken down from its altar, and, though stained and anti-aesthetic, it persistently receives the mechanical adoration of the devout, more for fear of innovation than due to true enthusiasm." [25] Thus, "Peronism" persists within the laboring classes, undoubtedly fomented by professional agitators and propagandists. Furthermore, in recent years workers have seen their real incomes shrink alarmingly. Most importantly, they have often found an enemy in government and, especially, the military. They have therefore lost the feeling that they are recognized and valued. They live in the perpetual fear that the old, *patrón-peón* days may return. Thus they cling to the *status quo,* to the old leaders and ideas, to the political labor movement, to the attainment of goals by decree and not by bargaining, to the fulfillment of short-run aims without too much consideration of the future. It is, however, significant to note that since the fall of the dictatorship, workers have not been able to act concertedly in the pursuit of their goals: today's labor movement is plagued by schism, confusion, and mistrust.

[25] Ramos Mejía, J. M.: *op. cit.,* p. 300.

We will suggest in our concluding chapter that in the long run, steady economic development is difficult to achieve without responsible, independent, democratic unions. These are characteristics which, in today's Argentina, are found only in very few unions, although unionism is undoubtedly strong. This is Perón's bitterest legacy, which includes an ever-deepening cleavage between government, labor, and employers. Steady economic development cannot be achieved unless some measure of willing co-operation between all sectors of the Argentine economy is achieved in the future. Maybe strong unions are necessary to insure such willing co-operation. But strength alone is by no means sufficient.

The political tendencies of Argentine trade-unionism may also have been fostered by the fact that the country has not enjoyed in the past a continuous period of political freedom. Argentine unions will not become nonpolitical until conditions of democracy are well established, *i.e.,* until unions can be certain that the existence of their organizations will be protected beyond the next *coup d'état*. Indeed, only a fair amount of democracy in the last couple of years has permitted the emergence of at least one largely nonpolitical bloc within the labor movement.[26]

But democracy is not enough. Labor's pervasive fear of exploitation, of nonrecognition, and of poverty must also disappear. Given the level of education and the cultural traits of the Argentine worker, the realization that such fears are ill-founded cannot come about by a worker's rational process. If labor is to co-operate responsibly in Argentina's economic development, *workers will have to be convinced* that they are expected to be responsible and reliable citizens, valued and indispensable members of a society whose very subsistence depends on the willing co-operation of all its members in furthering the common good. To achieve this goal, government's *co-operation* (rather than intervention) is obviously indispensable. But the main responsibility for its realization lies in Argentina's managerial force. It is clear that management's duty in the future, and at the same time its most difficult and important task, is the formation of a responsible working force. On it depends Argentina's future progress.

[26] See, for instance, U. S. Dept. of Labor: *op. cit.,* pp. 7–8 and 13–15.

6 THE FUTURE ROLE
OF INDUSTRIAL RELATIONS

A T THIS point, let us summarize the main concepts which have been presented in preceding chapters.

Steady economic development in Argentina cannot be reached *alone* by enlightened economic measures conducive in theory to a more rapid rise in per capita product and income. Such measures may certainly promote economic development for a short period, the extension of which is, for our purposes, irrelevant. Our theory is that unless the nation's *social development* is simultaneously fostered, economic gains achieved during one period will be largely wiped out in a following one by social or political dislocations. In other words, economic measures will be responsible for the creation of an *economic* environment sound enough to permit enterprising people to successfully carry out activities conducive to the nation's long-run progress. But unless such people exist in the first place; unless they are accepted, encouraged, and rewarded by other members of the society; unless the community is prepared to co-operate with them, *steady economic development cannot take place*. Social development is therefore indispensable to insure the *continuity* of economic development through time.

Our analyses of the causes, origins, and evolution of Argentine social shortcomings (from an economic-development point of view) have been summarized by suggesting that the Argentine society constitutes a "conglomeration" of individuals rather than a "community," a direct consequence of the basically passive, apathetic value orientations of its members. We have also suggested that it is the transformation of the Argentine society from its present form into a dynamic, organic community — *i.e.,* the development of the population's dominant value orientations towards higher degrees of activity — which is indispensable if steady economic development is to be insured. In this final chapter we will suggest that a new approach to industrial relations is the natural, indeed probably the only, way to achieve this goal.[1]

THE INSTITUTION OF CHANGE

According to what has been said of the Argentine "conglomeration" in preceding chapters, it is difficult to point out the factor or factors which cause the society to preserve its apparent unity. Some authors have suggested that it is the family which provides for it. Others seem to regard the state as the largely artificial institution without the existence of which the society would soon disintegrate. Furthermore, patriotism, nationalism, and the certainty of the nation's glorious destiny may have a powerful effect in holding together the Argentine "conglomeration."

Vertical social mobility and the rise of the middle sectors may also have had in the past a stabilizing effect upon the society. As has been already mentioned, however, we tend not to ascribe too much weight to the influence of the middle sectors in this respect, mainly because they are in themselves unstable, constituting anything but a compact social layer. This commentary also suggests that there is no reason to believe that the value orientations of middle-sector individuals differ greatly from those of the rest of the population. Their very lack of class-consciousness, coherence, and concerted political action is enough evidence in this respect. It is therefore clear that a change in the value-orientation profile of the society cannot be brought about by the conscious and deliberate choice of the bulk of the Argentine population. Regardless of the social layer to which they may belong, the problem is precisely that Argentines are unable to co-operate or to act concertedly in the common good. Furthermore, if they could "decide" to foster better understanding between the different sectors of the society, this would mean that they already possessed a community spirit, which is not true by assumption.

Therefore, the possibility of change can only depend upon the pres-

[1] In the conception and organization of ideas and notions presented in this chapter (and to some extent also in preceding ones), the author has been most influenced by the following works:

Banfield, E. C.: *The Moral Basis of a Backward Society* (Glencoe, Ill., The Free Press, 1958).

Hagen, E. E.: *How Economic Growth Begins: A Study in the Theory of Social Change* (Massachusetts Institute of Technology, 1959–60, mimeographed manuscript).

Harbison, F., and Myers, C. A.: *Management in the Industrial World,* Part I (New York, McGraw-Hill, 1959).

McGregor, D.: *The Human Side of Enterprise* (New York, McGraw-Hill, 1960).

Whyte, W. F., and Holmberg, A.: *Human Problems of U. S. Enterprise in Latin America, 1956* (Ithaca, N. Y., New York State School of Industrial and Labor Relations, Cornell University).

ence within the society of a minority group with the necessary ability, desire, knowledge, and prestige to plan for such change and to bring it about. The inclusion of prestige in the enumeration of necessary qualifications rules out the *direct* action of an outside (foreign) group of people as agents in the institution of change. And by "direct" we mean "direct contact" with the population. Foreign groups cannot lead because the nation will follow only a group which shares its cultural characteristics and whose leadership therefore does not seem to constitute a reflection on the worth and identity of the native society. This does not mean, however, that an *indirect* participation in this process of planned change may not be desirable or even necessary. We will suggest one such form of participation later in this chapter. In principle, however, prestige considerations circumscribe the enumeration of possible agents to bring about desired changes to Argentines themselves.

By no means do we consider the institution of necessary modifications easy or, without qualifications, at all possible. When we speak of "planned change," we do so mainly to simplify matters verbally. But there is no definitive evidence that the value-orientation profile *of a society* can be changed according to a preconceived scheme, although there is enough evidence that some degree of change in cognitive aspects of the "world view" of individuals or small groups can be achieved by plan.[2] There is also a fundamental difference between contriving consent and obedience through mass manipulation and propaganda methods, and changing a society's fundamental value-orientation profile. This is especially true if the evolution sought is in the direction of more rational and stern standards of conduct and ethics.

There are, however, certain boundaries to our problem which make us believe that a slow but effective process of change in the society's value-orientation profile may be induced in the future, based on many of those same cultural characteristics of the Argentine population which, unchecked, have led to the nation's economic stagnation.

In Chapter 2, we mentioned that Argentines are prone to follow those ways of action which they believe will maximize their short-run advantage. It may be therefore very difficult to induce Argentines to pursue a common goal which will not patently contribute in a reasonably short period of time to their own individual economic or social position in the society. The encouragement of co-operation in social, municipal, or charitable activities as a means of fostering the development of a community spirit seems therefore doomed to little success. On

---

[2] See, for instance, Schein, E.: "The Chinese Indoctrination Program for Prisoners of War: A Study of Attempted Brainwashing," in Maccoby, E. E., *et al.*: *Readings in Social Psychology,* 3rd Edition (New York, Henry Holt & Co., 1958), pp. 311–334.

the other hand, the society provides, and will increasingly do so, the ideal framework within which both goals — individual advantage and the creation of a spirit of co-operation — can be achieved at the same time: the industrial enterprise. In it, if a majority of individuals can be brought to recognize, by means of tangible proof and achievements, that private advantage can be greatly and rapidly fostered through active co-operation among all levels of the organization, the one goal (private advantage) would be achieved through the other (collective co-operation) rather than simultaneously. But the end product is certainly the same, with the added advantage that it would contribute materially and in a relatively short time to the nation's economic development. Needless to say, once the process is set in motion, it acquires a self-reinforcing character. Obviously, the whole problem lies in how to initiate such a process in an industrial organization.

The industrial enterprise presents further advantages as the framework within which a process of social change could be initiated. Provided that individual recognition of possible personal advantage through such a process exists, for co-operative action to occur it would not be necessary that passive value orientations be replaced overnight by idealism or altruism. Actually, *moderate* doses of selfishness, pride, and envy are valuable assets from the point of view of individual economic initiative. We speculate that if these and similar characteristics can be moderated by (as yet unspecified) managerial policies, the Argentine's proneness to follow ways of action that tend to maximize his short-run advantage must be considered a favorable factor in stimulating the development of more active value orientations and of more active patterns of economic activity.

The preceding paragraphs serve as an illustration for one of the principles which will guide our suggestions throughout this chapter and which should be helpful to those who, in the future, may undertake planned action conducive to the nation's social and economic development. The principle is that any scheme introduced in an attempt to influence value orientations should capitalize on existing cultural patterns rather than try to scrap them on grounds that they are the causes of past, objectionable effects. The consequences of the latter action upon the immediate stability of the society are obvious and impossible to check within the scope of a democratic state. Inconceivable as it may seem, however, this is the road which has been often followed in the past in an effort to solve the nation's social and political troubles.

Effect on Dominant Value Orientations

We have not yet stated explicitly why we believe that by achieving co-operation between individuals in an industrial enterprise, the society may develop a more active value-orientation profile. There is one reason which at first sight seems rather simple. Industry provides jobs to roughly one-third of the economically active Argentine population. If a considerable percentage of such people is induced by some method to collaborate with one another and if the effect of such co-operative efforts in industry is such as to induce other enterprises to follow the same scheme, the value orientations of the members of the society will have been (by definition) substantially changed. As we shall see, this simple explanation is, to say the least, illusory.

Fundamentally, the reason why industrial enterprises are the logical starting point of a gradual transformation of the Argentine society is not *only* the quantitative importance such establishments have and will increasingly acquire in the national economy. This is an undoubtedly important factor, but we believe that it is outweighed in importance by the fact that industry, and only industry, may be capable of supplying the enlightened leadership necessary to bring about the desired transformation. This point will be elaborated further below. We must anticipate, however, that such leaders will not appear overnight to change industry and the society, as if by magic. Change, if at all possible, may occur in more than a generation's time. It will be gradual and subject to the indecisions and partial failures of all trial-and-error types of modifications. But slowness is not a defect. It is the smallest price which Argentines will have to pay for past errors. Undoubtedly, the slower the process, the greater the danger of unexpected, extremist political action which would destroy the hopes for progress. But, at the same time, undue acceleration leads to a similar dead end.

Let us now suppose that in a considerable number of industrial enterprises, for one reason or another, an environment has been created in which: workers feel that they are recognized by their superiors; responsibilities and a certain degree of autonomy are *truly* delegated by all levels of management; all levels of personnel identify with their jobs, the enterprise, and its goals; workers willingly co-operate with each other and with all levels of management in the pursuit of personal, but common material advantages; individuals are free to discuss problems arising from their jobs with superiors and workmates and willingly take advantage of such opportunities. What will be the consequences of this still-hypothetical industrial environment? In the short run, it may substantially increase productivity in industry and thus foster economic development. On the other hand, however, *in the short run* it will *not* bring about a noticeable change in the *basic value orientations* of the people involved. But their anxiety, their rancor, their rage and forced suppression of it during working hours may have considerably declined. Workers may not have to consume most of their energy in the handling of inner conflicts. Above all, people will not need to discharge their anxiety, rage, and aggression on their subordinates and especially their *children,* since such feelings will have largely vanished. They may become more tractable, predictable, understanding, less autocratic fathers. Their verbalized or implicit attitudes at home towards manual work, industry, superiors, fellow workers, and unions may be more constructive and certainly show less anxiety attached to them. In accordance with the analysis developed in Chapter 2, this means that the individual's children are likely to develop a somewhat different, more active basic personality. Furthermore, if our hypothetical industrial environment develops and is adopted throughout large sectors of the nation's economy, the newly acquired value orientations and attitudes of our second-generation individual may fit and may be positively reinforced by his experience and perceptions of the outer world. Following the same line of reasoning expounded above, the probabilities that the third generation — our original individual's children's children — may develop more active value orientations are great.

As elsewhere in this book, elements of personality formation and factors affecting it have been here heroically simplified. We are, in fact, assuming that the incidence of factors external to the individual, his family, and his work place is either constant or irrelevant. We are also avoiding the consideration of other elements of personality formation which may mitigate or reinforce the process as pictured above. On the other hand, it seems reasonable to believe that the beneficial impact of our hypothetical industrial environment upon the overt attitudes and verbalized "world view" of the involved people will be of such importance that the family and social atmospheres in which their children will be brought up will be markedly different from those prevailing at present. This may indeed be a factor of much weight in the formation of more active basic personalities even if other, culturally patterned, child-rearing habits remain unmodified for a time.

If our exposition is correct, it may therefore take considerably more than a generation for the innovations applied in the field of industrial relations to have some effect on the society's value-orientation profile. On the other hand, during this "cultural lag" period, productivity in the industrial field will undoubtedly rise sharply. This contribution to the nation's immediate economic development may to some extent accelerate the process of cultural transformation.

Since Argentina is embarked — and rightly so — on a determined program of industrialization, the above-mentioned sequence of events seems to us the sole appropriate way to insure the success and continuity of Argentina's economic development. The creation of an industrial environment similar to the hypothetical model formerly depicted should therefore be the immediate goal of Argentine industrial enterprises. But, given the cultural characteristics of present-day Argentines, this goal cannot be expected to be achieved by the conscious and deliberate choice of the individuals involved. Nor can it be achieved by verbal exhortations and appeals to labor's patriotism and sense of responsibility. Argentina needs new leaders — not political but industrial leaders. They must have the moral capacity, training, foresight, and organizational creativity necessary to induce and guide their personnel, by means of material achievements and not through verbal exhortations alone, to accept willingly and co-operate actively within such a new industrial environment. Altruism need not necessarily be asked of these leaders. Indeed, they will largely be professional managers who are paid to lead. But whether they give leadership disinterestedly or see in it a road to personal advantage and prestige, they must be able to act responsibly in organizational roles; to be highly versatile and creative in personnel-administration matters; to inspire and maintain morale in their organizations; to *believe* in their subordinates; and to be in the highest degree conscious of the social implications of each of their decisions.

Means to an End

Briefly, the main task of future industrial leaders will be to eliminate the underlying conditions which produce the objectionable features of today's industrial environment and to create, instead, conditions which will "automatically," that is *without further direct interference by such leaders,* produce an environment consistent with the essential requirements of economic and social development. We have identified in earlier chapters those key elements causing unwanted effects to appear in industry. Some of the conditions which should be created have been enunciated in our description of the "ideal" industrial environment in the preceding section. We will now examine those managerial courses of action which we believe should lead to the realization of such an environment. The second important problem in this context — that is, the creation of a managerial force able and willing to put these or better suggestions into practice — will be discussed later in this section.

The Role of Management

Success or failure in the institution of a new, effective labor-management co-operation climate in the enterprise depends entirely on the attitudes towards one another of the parties concerned. Therefore, and assuming for the time being that top management indeed possesses the proper attitude towards labor, Argentine entrepreneurs will initially face the same problem other employers throughout the world have met in the past and will continue to face in the future: the positive motivation of the work force. There exist many techniques in the field of personnel administration which have been used in industrially advanced countries to achieve such motivation and to foster labor-management understanding and collaboration. The direct transposition of such techniques, without giving due attention to cultural differences between Argentine workers and those of other countries, may prove dangerous. One failure due to a lack of adaptation of one such technique to local requirements may forever discredit participative schemes in the particular enterprise. On the other hand, the personnel-administration philosophies underlying many of those techniques seem to us to be of direct application in Argentina. In other words, there is no reason to believe that Argentine workers have basically different attitudes toward their jobs from workers anywhere else in industrialized Western countries.

Let us further elaborate this point. We think that workers are more likely to co-operate with management if the reasons for management action are *explained* to them. We believe that the productivity of Argentine workers will greatly increase if they enjoy their daily work, if they identify themselves with it and with the goals of the enterprise, if they are permitted some degree of *participation* in the process of deciding on matters which directly affect them and their jobs. This has certainly not been the rule in Argentine industry ever since its initial development more than half a century ago. Workers have been consistently denied initiative and responsibilities by an extreme centralization of decision-making within the enterprise, by an authoritarian system of supervision extending through all managerial levels, and by the excessive functionalization of production techniques following theories which Argentine managers still consider to be conducive to highest labor productivity. We think that workers, if properly encouraged by management, will make effective use of opportunities to take responsibilities and exercise initiative, provided that they recognize in such approach a *sincere* effort by management to improve the workers' lot.

We must, however, recognize that a worker who possesses passive value orientations, high need dependency, a strong need aggression — and who has visualized his employer as an enemy and made him the focus of his rage and aggressive drives — may not want to co-operate with management in the creation of a participative enterprise environment. Not only would he be thus collaborating with an enemy, but he would feel insecure in a new environment where decisions are largely not made for him and which therefore does not satisfy his need dependency. In our judgment, however, these negative influences should be outweighed by the fulfillment of the worker's drive for recognition; by the material rewards participation will undoubtedly bring to him; and especially by the fact that by following the lead of obviously successful members of the native society who — he therefore assumes — share with him the society's cultural characteristics, the worker is pursuing personal advantages without unconsciously violating his sense of identity and individual worth. Again, this is obviously only possible provided that management's efforts to secure workers' co-operation are *sincere* — that is, totally devoid of any recognizable attitude of condescension with regard to the working force and its problems.

Furthermore, to encourage the development of people able and willing to exercise initiative, to make the identification of worker and job at all possible, management must decentralize its administrative functions, it must be willing to delegate authority and responsibilities, and it must also avoid excessive functionalization of the techniques of production. In new industries or new enterprises, early stages of development may naturally require close supervision at all levels of the undertaking because of the lack of skilled personnel. This early stage of close supervision, however, should be regarded as one in which superiors primarily *train* rather than supervise. They should *explain* why certain methods are used and their relationship to the whole undertaking, rather than apply the assuredly easier but, in the long run, costlier method of simply ordering their subordinates to do something.

The effective motivation of the working force therefore depends not only on a proper attitude of top management towards labor but also upon the transmission of this attitude through middle management to supervisors. Delegation of authority and responsibilities and, at the same time, the assignment of clearly defined functions to the middle and lower management hierarchy will certainly facilitate such a process. But it appears also that continued education at all levels is fundamental to bringing about a satisfactory solution to these problems.

It may be necessary to clarify that by advising decentralization we are far from suggesting, especially at early stages, anything approaching the notion of "management by objectives." [3] Nor are we suggesting that top management will face fewer responsibilities than is presently the case. On the contrary, our notion of decentralization entails the delegation of authority, not of *control*. Indeed, it has been the experience of United States enterprises that the more top management tries to decentralize

[3] Drucker, P.: *The Practice of Management* (New York, Harper & Bros., 1954), Chapter 11. See also Harbison, F., and Myers, C. A.: *op. cit.*, pp. 41–43; and McGregor, D.: *op. cit.*, esp. pp. 61–76.

decision-making, the more it must centralize its control of decisions. The task of top management should be one of co-ordination, broad decision-making, and control, rather than the time- and energy-consuming administration of petty, routine matters still common in Argentine enterprises. *Decentralization is no substitute for leadership, but an implementation of it.*

Moreover, from a personnel-administration viewpoint, the type of management we are here considering is indeed extremely difficult to achieve:

> Securing "participation" of the work force must strike a precarious balance between a pretense of participation, which will arouse distrust and antagonism, and too much participation, when everybody is happy but unified direction is lost. Successful motivation of the work force appears most often to require the effective exercise of leadership in a democratic setting where leadership is based largely on consent. Managerial skills of high order are required, not only at the top, but throughout the managerial hierarchy.[4]

In the past, Argentine managements have attempted to motivate the working force to higher degrees of productivity and "loyalty" through the institution of incentive schemes. Some of the results obtained have been presented in connection with our discussion of the productivity of the Argentine labor force.

At first sight, these results seem indeed startling. In our opinion, however, great care must be taken in drawing rash conclusions as to the apparent usefulness of such incentive schemes. At the time they were instituted, both productivity and real wages were at a very low level, so that in the short run the prospect of fat bonuses and the relative ease with which they could be earned may have outweighed other, negative effects on the working force. There are good grounds, however, for believing that in the long run a system of *individual* incentives is inimical to the development of the co-operative environment we have deemed essential to the nation's economic and social progress.

As has already been mentioned in Chapter 5, each individual needs to see his behavior validated by the acceptance of it by his "reference group." In the industrial situation, a worker's reference group is his workmates. Individual incentives reward a type of behavior that is disapproved of by a worker's reference group. This is especially true in Argentina, given the cultural attitude of basic distrust towards other individuals. Therefore the individual's rewards and punishments point in opposite

---

[4] Harbison, F., and Myers, C. A.: *op. cit.,* p. 32.

directions at the same time.[5] This may subject the individual to a situation of internal, emotional conflict which will increase his anxiety while undermining his energy and thus his efficiency. Furthermore, even if a new situation of equilibrium is reached within the group, it will be at the cost of an increase in the group's inner tensions. In other words, individual incentives may cause further impairment of those objectionable features that management should, by assumption, seek to eliminate.

On the other hand, we suggest that carefully devised schemes of *collective participation* in the planning and furtherance of production, and in the added profits derived therefrom,[6] would be extremely helpful in encouraging the gradual achievement of an appropriate industrial environment.

Some of the main advantages we have in mind are the following:

(1) the encouragement of *co-operation* between all levels of the organization, from top management down to maintenance workers, with immediate and tangible proof that such co-operation *pays* in term of higher productivity, higher profits, and higher wages;

(2) the realization that all elements in the organization — management, manual workers, and administrative personnel included — can and *do* play a very important role in the furtherance of the common (and at the same time personal) interest; to a certain extent, this last feature may relieve the people from the stigma of manual work;

(3) increased understanding of the problems and needs *of other people* and the realization that only a *common effort* — and not luck or divine grace — can and does lead to success and well-being;

(4) finally, the realization by superiors at all levels that their subordinates are mostly responsible people, capable of high job performances, if only given the measure of trust and self-respect the superior asks for himself.

At the risk of being monotonous, two warnings should be repeated. First, great care must be taken not to attempt to transpose directly schemes evolved and successfully applied in other, industrially advanced countries. But if carefully adapted to Argentine requirements, cultural conditions, and educational standards, such plans will certainly prove to be of great value. Second, unless management *sincerely believes* in such schemes

---

[5] See also Whyte, W. F.: "The Individual and Behavior Change" in *Human Problems of U. S. Enterprise in Latin America, 1957* (Ithaca, N. Y., New York State School of Industrial and Labor Relations, Cornell University), pp. 56–58.

[6] See, for instance, Lesieur, F. (ed.): *The Scanlon Plan. . . . A Frontier in Labor-Management Cooperation* (published for the M.I.T. Industrial Relations Section by the Technology Press, Massachusetts Institute of Technology, and John Wiley & Sons, Inc., New York, 1958).

and in its underlying philosophy towards the personnel, the institution of any such plan is bound to be fruitless. More important than the plan itself is management's attitude towards the work force and its perseverance in encouraging the co-operation of its personnel. The initial response of labor to any such suggestion may well be negative, as a consequence of the workers' distrust in employers. It lies in management's ability to seek the collaboration of unions in devising co-operation plans, so as to iron out such difficulties.

The general approach of management towards unions is certainly a complex question. It is in the interest of long-run economic growth to encourage the formation and development of independent, democratic unions. Only under such conditions will unions willingly and responsibly co-operate with management. Here again, management must find an adequate balance between the overt promotion of responsible unions and objectionable intervention in the affairs of organized labor. At any rate, the organization of "company unions" is undesirable because they constitute an attempt to perpetuate the authoritarian management system within a "constitutional" industrial-relations framework. Company unions should therefore be avoided in the interest of *steady, long-run* economic development. This view has been well expressed by S. Romualdi:

> They might give a temporary illusion of peace, but company unions will sooner or later be taken over by discontented elements with results not always satisfactory. If you [management] have a legitimate union in existence, after five or ten years, by the process of natural selection, you are going to have a group of trained leaders who begin to understand the role of a union in cooperating with management, at least in the technical sense of this expression. But you may have a company union for fifty years, and at the end of fifty years you still will have no single person who is strong enough to speak on behalf of the workers. "Yes-men" are not the people you need. A company union is often able to fill the ranks with 90 or 100 percent membership but the leaders of a company union are not trusted, are not liked by the members and are not listened to in times of crisis.[7]

Management should also undertake the responsibility of extending and perfecting existing vocational training schemes — which in Argentina are often set up by contractual arrangements between unions and employers — in an effort to improve the skills of the work force and encourage the gradual development of some measure of pride in those workers who possess particular skills and workmanship abilities. Measures to improve

[7] "Problems of Union-Management Relations in Latin America," in *Human Problems of U. S. Enterprise in Latin America, 1957* (Ithaca, N. Y., New York School of Industrial and Labor Relations, Cornell University), p. 8.

the general educational level of workers will certainly have the interest and support of organized labor. As has already been mentioned, formal education has always been an avenue for social mobility. To have it open to him will surely give the worker the sense of being a valued member of the society.

Development of Managerial Resources

Through the preceding pages we have assumed the availability of a managerial force able and willing to put our suggestions into practice. Clearly, the fundamental factor on which the realization of our suggestions depends is the existence of such a managerial force. It is also clear that for managers to decentralize operations, delegate authority, and encourage workers' participation in the affairs of the enterprise, it is necessary that they be no longer unconsciously controlled by the Argentine national character. In other words, they must possess somewhat more active cultural characteristics than the rest of the society (outright social rebels would certainly be alienated by it), and an intellectual capacity and education high enough to consciously understand, accept, and carry out the role they will be called on to play in the long-overdue development of a modern industrial society.

In the concluding paragraphs of Chapters 2 and 4, we expressed a hopeful opinion regarding the current existence of appropriate "raw material" out of which such a new élite of enlightened professional managers could be shaped. But we lack the empirical evidence definitely to assert whether or not the Argentine society is presently producing such an "out-group" of individuals who, having reason to be dissatisfied, possess personality traits which would spur them to the achievement of their goals, and to the sublimation of their antagonism towards the customary power-holders in the society, by pushing forward as entrepreneurs. Whether this is true or false, however, it is certain that in the future more and more university graduates — that is, people with an education and, supposedly, intellectual abilities markedly above the society's average — will find in the field of industrial management the most rewarding professional careers open to them. With the exception of those students who may choose medical or other sciences not directly applicable to industry, the culturally patterned drive to obtain an academic degree plus a growing supply of professional management positions will contribute to the *natural* selection of the most capable and ambitious members of the society for industry.

If the preceding considerations are correct, the emergence of what we have called an "enlightened management minority" depends only on the opportunities Argentines may be given to familiarize themselves thoroughly with the theories, practice, and tools of management; and with the social, economic, and political implications of economic development. Although creative entrepreneurship in the technology aspects of industry is essential to economic development, Argentina also needs versatile, imaginative innovators in the field of industrial and public relations. Therefore, besides a qualified technical education, future managers should be thoroughly exposed to all those social problems which are likely to arise through a process of industrialization and economic development *in Argentina.*

There are several roads open to the development of Argentine managerial resources. One road available is the participation of foreign capital in such development. Foreign investments in Argentina should certainly be encouraged, but with the understanding that foreign investors will guarantee to train or accept experienced nationals for managerial positions. A monopoly or continued control of such positions by foreigners, and the identification by Argentines of industry with alien value orientations and attitudes which would follow, would destroy all hopes for the kind of social change we deem necessary to insure steady economic growth. As has been suggested in our analysis of immigrant acculturation in Chapter 2, in the past the Argentine society defended itself when faced with a similar situation by compulsively clinging to its traditional value-orientation profile.

The direct importation of engineers, scientists, and professional managers from abroad to serve in Argentine enterprises may be necessary to help start new industries, state and private, and to train native counterparts in such enterprises. Apart from such cases, however, such a policy may not actually warrant the high costs involved, especially because such people may not be able to fulfill their mission effectively as a result of the negative attitude which Argentines (both management and especially labor) would adopt towards them. On the other hand, the importation of foreign professors or lecturers to teach courses in management, engineering, and applied sciences would seem to be of incalculable value. Similarly, Argentine industry and government should materially encourage the training of nationals abroad. Here again, the high cost involved in such programs is a serious barrier to an effective utilization of this educational resource.

Undoubtedly, the best long-run investment is the development of a high-talent managerial force *at home.* This is a task of both private industry and government. At the private level, this means executive-development programs and training of lower managerial cadres *on the job,* willingness to delegate authority and responsibility to lower managerial ranks, and the staffing of managerial positions on the basis of ability rather than kinship. On the other hand, the state should take advantage of its centralized control over the nation's educational system to encourage, guide, and supervise the education and training of future managerial cadres. A first-class managerial hierarchy cannot be developed without specialized industrial-management programs, modern technological institutions, and competent teaching staffs. The Argentine educational system is to a large extent geared to the formation of professionals who fail to enter economically directly productive activities. Economic-development objectives call for a shift of such emphasis towards the development of professionals trained in engineering, applied sciences, and industrial management.

The Role of Government

Finally, we need to consider briefly the future role of government in industrial relations. To fulfill the goals of economic and social development, the co-operation of government is essential. Co-operation, however, does not mean intervention. If employers and labor are to develop from within their ranks creative, innovative members, individuals able and willing to exercise initiative and contribute responsibly to the common, long-run welfare, their actions should not be constantly hampered by governmental measures which, more often than not, are apt to be arbitrary and subject to be declared void on short notice. Long-run economic-development objectives make it essential for government to encourage the development of responsible citizens. This cannot be achieved if the Presidency governs by decree. Centralization in government breeds centralization in all sectors of the national life, industry and labor included.

Of course, decentralization cannot take place overnight, lest serious dislocations occur. The process should be gradual, but steady. At least during the next few years, the centralized power now used to frustrate private action should be used to promote it. Instead of approving or disapproving private measures in industry on purely political grounds as has been customary in the past, government might make use of its present power to make progress towards responsible, co-operative labor-management action in the public interest a condition of approval. Obviously, we have collective-bargaining procedures especially in mind, but the same principle could be applied to the establishment of voluntary arbitration boards, productivity committees, apprenticeship programs, employment services, recreational and health facilities, and similar schemes. The centralized power of government could also be usefully applied to the betterment and reorganization of the Argentine higher-education system, as suggested earlier, and to make it more readily available to all (income and geographical) sectors of the population.

Another area of industrial relations where governmental action could greatly implement the general measures we have suggested is that of labor legislation and social welfare. It has been remarked with ample justification that "the activity of legislative bodies in Latin America is often in inverse proportion to the ability to put the legislation into effect." [8] Argentina does not escape from this criticism. Acquiring status as the champion of labor, Perón was quick to point out that much of the labor legislation enacted before 1943 had never been really administered or enforced. This was no doubt true, but after the fall of the dictatorship the new government found that standards of application continued to fall short of standards of legislation, particularly as they concerned the fulfillment of obligations by the state. On the other hand, strict enforcement was the rule against private "anti-Peronist" employers and foreign-owned enterprises. Enforcement of legislation has usually depended upon the influence that labor, employer, or other groups may have had with the particular administration. Today, the situation is greatly complicated because neither government nor the National Social Welfare Institute (under whose jurisdiction all national pension funds are grouped) has sufficient means to fulfill its obligations promptly and regularly.[9] Furthermore, because of distances and lack of control, enforcement of labor legislation in rural areas has been usually less effective than in the cities.

In general, therefore, the main barrier to a satisfactory enforcement of labor legislation has been the lack of a well-trained, politically independent body of public servants. This has meant that legislation enacted at the urgent demands of the workers has very often failed to produce better living and working conditions. More seriously, however, the proliferation of laws without effective administration reflects the lack of a sincere and realistic understanding of labor and industrial-relations problems on the part of employers and government.[10] On the other hand, in many instances the employer has been absolutely unable to meet the expense involved in some of the benefit schemes accorded to the worker by the law.

[8] Hanson, S.: *Economic Development in Latin America* (Washington, D. C., The Inter-American Affairs Press, 1951), p. 498.

[9] See also *La Razón* (Buenos Aires, Sept. 25, 1959), p. 6; and U. S. Department of Labor: *Foreign Labor Information — Labor in Argentina* (Washington, D. C., Bureau of Labor Statistics, June 1959), pp. 21–22. In 1959, the state owed the Social Welfare Institute more than 52 billion pesos.

[10] Pierson, W., and Gil, F.: *Governments of Latin America* (New York, McGraw-Hill, 1957), pp. 371–372.

Such cases of government or employer inability to fulfill social obligations make it logical to wonder whether excessively advanced social-security schemes are at all beneficial to the country's long-run social and economic progress. If high profits are the basis for the expansion of capital accumulation, and if Professor Joseph Spengler is right in suggesting that industrial progress is markedly dependent upon the degree to which imaginative and energetic entrepreneurs "are free of hampering and institutional arrangements," [11] then excessive social-security obligations in Argentina may be hindering economic development and thus preventing the attainment of higher standards of living. This of course does not mean that Argentina should go backward in repealing established schemes. Politically and socially, this would be sheer folly. The point simply is that labor's efforts should in the future concentrate on securing higher wages and not on gaining further social benefits which, instead of contributing to the workers' sense of security, might well lead to the long-run stagnation of their living standards. Therefore, it would be extremely helpful if government took advantage of its current power to see to it that in future bargaining sessions real (not merely inflationary) labor gains were realized in the form of higher wages rather than in increased social benefits. Since this would be to the benefit of workers and entrepreneurs alike, management should also try to abide by this policy.

Finally, government, beyond insuring that democratic practices prevail in the election and control of officials by the membership, should keep its hands off union affairs. We recognize that this may represent mere wishful thinking. In a country like Argentina, it is still extremely difficult for a political party to win a Presidential election without at least the approval of labor. This establishes a community of interest which cannot be easily destroyed without endangering the stability of the nation. More importantly, it may be true that *rapid* economic growth is not possible without government-controlled unions. Such an approach, however, defeats its own purpose. The same commentaries we quoted in our discussion of "company unions" apply here. "Puppet" unions may facilitate short-run economic gains. But *steady, long-run* economic growth can only be achieved with a responsible, independent, democratic labor movement. He who needs proof should recall that Argentina collapsed economically during the only period in its history in which government completely controlled the labor movement, and this occurred in spite of tangible economic achievements during initial years (up until 1948).

[11] Spengler, J.: "Economic Factors in the Development of Densely Populated Areas," in *Proceedings of the American Philosophical Society* (February 1951), p. 22.

Conclusion

The current inadequacy of Argentine industrial relations is basically a manifestation of the lack of "co-operation-mindedness" or "community spirit" within the Argentine society, and this feature itself is only one manifestation of a wider social problem — what we would like to call *the* "Argentine problem": a value-orientation profile which is inimical to the nation's long-run economic growth. If we chose Argentine industrial relations as the framework of these three concluding chapters, it was because we believe that owing to the future course which the Argentine economy *must* take if the nation is to progress and develop, *the solution of the "Argentine problem" can and must be reached by the suggested solution of the industrial-relations problem.* This statement needs to be clarified in two respects:

First, we do by no means contend that one element *alone* is the cause of the nation's current period of economic stagnation. In addition to the social problem that we have discussed throughout this work, there are other economic, political, and social impediments of considerable importance. The viewpoint we have taken here is that the basically passive value-orientation profile of the Argentine society is the *critical,* or *fundamental,* factor which prevents the nation from accomplishing steady economic growth.

Second, we do not contend that the solution of Argentina's economic-development problem lies in the suggested solution of its industrial-relations problem *alone.* The problem of Argentina's economic development must be attacked *on all fronts,* economic and political as well as social. It is our contention, however, that the solution of Argentina's social problem is a *sine qua non* to make long-run economic development possible. Purely economic measures may to a large extent govern the *speed* and *rate* of economic development in Argentina—but not its *continuity.* Only a transformation of Argentina's value-orientation profile towards higher degrees of activity can insure that economic gains achieved during one period will not be wiped out in a following one by social and political dislocations.

Up to the present, industrialization in Argentina has been retarded by largely noneconomic factors. What we mean by this can be best explained by considering what successful industrialization involves. Fundamentally, successful industrialization depends not only on a considerable degree of geographical mobility in the industrial labor force but also, and more importantly, on occupational mobility, a maximum utilization of specialized skills, and generally on the psychological commitment of management, labor, and the community at large to the aims and goals of industrialization and economic-development programs: *a steady rise in per capita output and the balanced distribution of the steadily rising per capita income among all sectors of the population.*

By "steady," we mean essentially "continuous over the long run," since *moderate* cyclical fluctuations seem unavoidable and even necessary to insure an effective utilization and interplay of all factors of production. Indeed, the general approach to all problems discussed in this work, and especially in this last chapter, has been essentially a *long-run* one. Actually, if all the measures which have been suggested here were put into practice promptly and effectively, no *dramatic* improvement in the nation's economic position would ensue unless the state followed economic policies conducive to rapid economic growth.

On the other hand, even enlightened governmental measures would not insure long-run economic development unless the social measures we have suggested are carried out actively and without further delay. Under the most favorable conditions it might take two or three generations for the new industrial environment to exert lasting effect on the dominant value orientations of the society at large. Therefore, it is essential to the future progress of Argentina that measures conducive to the creation of a new, co-operative industrial-relations climate be urgently undertaken.

BIBLIOGRAPHY

A. *General*

Banfield, Edward C.: *The Moral Basis of a Backward Society*. Glencoe, Ill., The Free Press, 1958.

Drucker, Peter F.: *The Practice of Management*. New York, Harper & Bros., 1954.

Freud, Anna: *The Ego and the Mechanisms of Defence*. New York. International Universities Press, Inc., 11th Printing, 1960.

Hagen, Everett E.: *How Economic Growth Begins: A Study in the Theory of Social Change*. Massachusetts Institute of Technology, 1959–1960 (mimeographed manuscript).

Hanson, Simon G.: *Economic Development in Latin America*. Washington, D. C., The Inter-American Affairs Press, 1951.

Harbison, Frederick, and Myers, Charles A.: *Management in the Industrial World*. New York, McGraw-Hill, 1959.

Harris, Seymour E. (ed.): *Economic Problems of Latin America*. New York, McGraw-Hill, 1944.

Higgins, Benjamin: *Economic Development*. New York, W. W. Norton & Co., 1959.

Institute of International Industrial and Labor Relations, Cornell University: *Labor, Management, and Economic Growth*, edited by Robert L. Aronson and John P. Windmuller. Ithaca, N. Y., 1954.

International Labour Office: *Report of the Director-General*, Report I, Part I, International Labour Conference, Forty-third Session. Geneva, 1959.

Kahl, Joseph A.: "Some Social Concomitants of Industrialization and Urbanization." *Human Organization*, Vol. 18, No. 2, pp. 53–74.

Kardiner, Abram, *et al.*: *The Psychological Frontiers of Society*. New York, Columbia University Press, 1945.

Kindleberger, Charles P.: *Economic Development*. New York, McGraw-Hill, 1958.

Kluckhohn, Florence R., "Dominant and Variant Value Orientations," in Kluckhohn, Murray, and Schneider (eds.): *Personality in Nature, Society and Culture*, 2nd ed., rev. and enl. (New York, Alfred A. Knopf, 1955), Chapter 21.

Lesieur, Frederick G. (ed.): *The Scanlon Plan, A Frontier in Labor-Management Cooperation*. Published jointly by The Technology Press of the Massachusetts Institute of Technology and John Wiley & Sons, Inc., New York, 1958.

Maccoby, E. E.; Newcomb, T. M.; and Hartley, E. L. (eds.): *Readings in Social Psychology*. New York, Henry Holt & Co., 1958.

McGregor, Douglas: *The Human Side of Enterprise.* New York, McGraw-Hill, 1960.

Merton, Robert K.: *Social Theory and Social Structure,* rev. and enl. Glencoe, Ill., The Free Press. 1957.

New York State School of Industrial and Labor Relations, Cornell University: *Human Problems of United States Enterprise in Latin America, 1957.* Ithaca, N. Y., 1957.

Piers, Gerhard, and Singer, Milton B.: *Shame and Guilt.* Springfield, Ill., Charles C. Thomas, 1953.

Redfield, Robert: *Peasant Society and Culture.* Chicago, University of Chicago Press, 1956.

Rostow, W. W.: *The Process of Economic Growth.* New York, W. W. Norton & Company, Inc., 1952.

Schein, Edgar H.: *Interpersonal Communication, Group Solidarity, and Social Influence.* Massachusetts Institute of Technology, unpublished address delivered to the International Council for Women Psychologists on August 28, 1958 (Washington, D. C.).

Spengler, Joseph J.: "Economic Factors in the Development of Densely Populated Areas," in *Proceedings of the American Philosophical Society.* February 1951.

Teichert, Pedro C. M.: *Economic Policy Revolution and Industrialization in Latin America.* Bureau of Business Research, University, Miss., University of Mississippi, 1959.

United Nations: *Report on the World Social Situation.* New York, 1957.

———— : Department of Economic and Social Affairs: *Processes and Problems of Industrialization in Under-Developed Countries.* New York, 1955.

———— : Economic Commission for Latin America, *The Latin American Common Market.* New York, 1959.

Whyte, William F., and Holmberg, Allan R.: *Human Problems of U. S. Enterprise in Latin America, 1956.* Ithaca, N. Y., New York State School of Industrial and Labor Relations, Cornell University.

B. *Argentina (general)*

Alexander, Robert J.: *Communism in Latin America* (New Brunswick, N. J., Rutgers University Press, 1957), Chapter IX.

———— : *The Peron Era.* New York, Columbia University Press, 1951.

Blanksten, George I.: *Peron's Argentina.* The University of Chicago Press, 1953.

Bruce, James: *Those Perplexing Argentines.* New York, Longmans, Green & Co., 1953.

Defelippe, Bruno A.: *Geografía Económica Argentina.* Buenos Aires, Ed. Losange, 1959.

Di Tella, Guido J. M.: *Economic History of Argentina; 1914–1933.* Ph.D. thesis, Massachusetts Institute of Technology, 1960 (unpublished).

Estrada, José Manuel: *La Política Liberal bajo la Tiranía de Rosas.* Published as Vol. LXXXIII in the series Grandes Escritores Argentinos, Alberto Palcos, ed., Buenos Aires, 1925.

Germani, Gino: *Estructura Social de la Argentina.* Buenos Aires, Ed. Raigal, 1955.

———— : "Algunas Repercusiones Sociales de los Cambios Económicos en la Argentina," in *Cursos y Conferencias.* Buenos Aires, Jan.–March 1952, summarized in *Ciencias Sociales,* Pan American Union, Vol. III, No. 18 (Dec. 1952), pp. 147–158

Hanke, Lewis: *South America* (Princeton, N. J., D. Van Nostrand Co., Inc., 1959), pp. 58–76, and 150–165.

James, Preston E.: *Latin America,* 3rd ed. (New York, The Odyssey Press, 1959), Chapter 9.

Johnson, John J.: *Political Change in Latin America* (Stanford, Cal., Stanford University Press, 1958), esp. Chapter 6.

Kennedy, John J.: *Catholicism, Nationalism, and Democracy in Argentina.* Notre Dame, Ind., University of Notre Dame Press, 1958.

Mallea, Eduardo: *Historia de una Pasión Argentina.* Buenos Aires, Espasa-Calpe, 1945.

Murena, H. A.: "Notas sobre la Crisis Argentina," in *Sur,* No. 248 (Buenos Aires, 1957), pp. 1–16. Partially transcribed in Hanke, L.: *op. cit.,* pp. 160–161.

Ortega y Gasset, José: "Intimidades" in *Obras Completas,* 3rd ed., 2 vols. (Madrid, Espasa-Calpe S. A., 1943), pp. 654–681.

Ortiz, Ricardo M.: *Historia Económica de la Argentina,* 2 vols. Buenos Aires, Ed. Raigal, 1955.

Pendle, George: *Argentina.* London, Oxford University Press, 1955.

Pierson, William W., and Gil, Federico G.: *Governments of Latin America.* New York, McGraw-Hill, 1957.

Ramos Mejía, José M.: *Las Multitudes Argentinas.* Buenos Aires, G. Kraft Ltda., 1952.

República Argentina, Comisión Nacional de la Vivienda: *Plan de Emergencia, Informe Elevado al Poder Ejecutivo Nacional.* Buenos Aires, April 1956.

———— : Dirección Nacional de Industrias del Estado: *Reseña de las Actividades del Organismo.* Buenos Aires, Ministerio de Industria y Comercio de la Nación, April 1958.

Sarmiento, Domingo F.: *Facundo: Civilización y Barbarie.* Universidad Nacional de La Plata, Alberto Palcos (ed.), 1938.

Scalabrini Ortiz, Raúl: *Historia de los Ferrocarriles Argentinos.* Buenos Aires, Editorial Devenir, 1957.

Taylor, Carl C.: *Rural Life in Argentina.* Louisiana State University Press, 1948.

United Nations, C.E.P.A.L.: *Economic Bulletin for Latin America,* Vol. IV, No. 1 (Santiago, Chile, March 1959), pp. 13–24.

———— : *El Desarrollo Económico de la Argentina* (Vol. V of Análisis y Proyecciones del Desarrollo Económico), Part I. Mexico, 1959.

——— : *Estudio Económico de América Latina, 1957* (Mexico, September 1958), esp. pp. 115–134.

Whitaker, Arthur P.: *The United States and Argentina.* Cambridge, Mass., Harvard University Press, 1954.

Zymelman, Manuel: *The Economic History of Argentina (1933–1952).* Ph.D. thesis, Massachusetts Institute of Technology, 1958 (unpublished).

C. *Argentine Labor and Labor Legislation*

Antokoletz, Daniel: *Derecho del Trabajo y Previsión Social,* 2 vols., 2nd ed. Buenos Aires, G. Kraft Ltda., 1953.

Argimón, Carlos R.: *Relaciones del Trabajo y Colaboración en la Empresa.* Buenos Aires, G. Kraft Ltda., 1954.

Belaúnde, César H.: *Los Convenios Colectivos de Trabajo en la Argentina.* Buenos Aires, Selección Contable, 1958.

Bidart Campos, Germán J.: *El Régimen Nacional de Previsión Social.* Buenos Aires, Editorial Alfa, 1958.

Deveali, Mario L.: *Curso de Derecho Sindical y de la Previsión Social.* Buenos Aires, Víctor P. de Zavalía, 1954.

Garzón Ferreyra, Ignacio: *La Convención Colectiva de Trabajo.* Buenos Aires, Ed. Arayú, 1954.

Krotoschin, Ernesto: *Curso de Legislación del Trabajo.* Buenos Aires, Editorial Depalma, 1950.

——— : *Tratado Práctico de Derecho del Trabajo,* 2 vols. Buenos Aires, Editorial Depalma, 1955.

Librería "El Ateneo" (ed.): *Estudios de Derecho del Trabajo en Memoria de Alejandro M. Unsain.* Buenos Aires, 1954.

Palacios, Alfredo L.: *La Defensa del Valor Humano,* Buenos Aires, Ed. Claridad, 1939.

——— : *La Justicia Social.* Buenos Aires, Ed. Claridad, 1954.

Pan American Union: *Labor Trends and Social Welfare in Latin America, 1941 and 1942* (Washington, D. C., July 1943), Chapter I.

República Argentina, Ministerio de Trabajo y Seguridad Social: *Convenios Colectivos de Trabajo.* Buenos Aires, Dirección Nacional de Estadística y Censos, 1958.

Ruprecht, Alfredo O. J.: *Evolución de la Legislación Nacional del Trabajo.* Buenos Aires, Ed. Bibliográfica Argentina, 1951.

Sylvester, Hugo L.: *Régimen del Trabajo Rural.* Buenos Aires, Ed. Claridad, 1951.

Tieffenberg, David: *Exigencias Proletarias a la Revolución* and *La Legislación Obrera en el Régimen Peronista.* Buenos Aires, Ediciones Populares Argentinas, 1956.

United States Department of Labor, Bureau of Labor Statistics: *Foreign Labor Information — Labor in Argentina.* Washington, D. C., June 1959.

Unsain, Alejandro M.: *Legislación del Trabajo.* Buenos Aires, Ed. Abeledo, 1925.

———— : *Ordenamiento de las Leyes Obreras Argentinas,* 4th ed. Buenos Aires, Ed. El Ateneo, 1952.

Vernengo, Roberto: "Freedom of Association and Industrial Relations in Latin America," Parts I (pp. 451 ff.) and II (pp. 592 ff.) in *International Labour Review,* Vol. 73, 1956.

D. *Periodicals*

International Labour Office, *Legislative Series* (quarterly), Argentina.
International Labour Review, Geneva.
————, *Statistical Supplement,* Geneva.
La Prensa, Buenos Aires.
La Razón, Buenos Aires.
República Argentina, *Boletín Oficial,* Buenos Aires.
Time Magazine.

INDEX